Also by Lewis Burke Frumkes
How to Raise Your I.Q. by Eating Gifted Children

The Mensa Think-Smart Book, with Dr. Abbie Salny

Name Crazy

MANHATTAN COCKTAIL

and other
Irreverent Observations on Life,
Taxes, and Meter Maids

Lewis
Burke
Frumkes

A Fireside Book
Published by Simon & Schuster Inc.
New York·London·Toronto·Sydney·Tokyo

F

Fireside
Simon & Schuster Building
Rockefeller Center
1230 Avenue of the Americas
New York, New York 10020

Designed by Julie Duquet
Manufactured in the United States of America

10   9   8   7   6   5   4   3   2   1

Library of Congress Cataloging in Publication Data
Frumkes, Lewis Burke.
   Manhattan cocktail : and other irreverent obser-
vations on life, taxes, and meter maids / Lewis
Burke Frumkes.
       p.   cm.
   "A Fireside book."
   I. Title.
PN6162.F78   1989
814'.54—dc20   89–34732
ISBN 0-671-67142-1   CIP

For Yussel, who would have enjoyed this book.

ACKNOWLEDGMENTS

Tim McGinnis, from the first, until the end, was my advocate, my inspired editor, and my friend. I will always owe him a debt of gratitude. I wish to express special thanks also to Laura Yorke, my bright, talented, and impossibly optimistic editor, and to Robin Rue, my loyal and canny agent, who for some ungodly reason thinks I am a riot. I believe it has to do with the fact that she once played the drums in a rock group. It's out now Robin, Pandora made me do it. And finally, thanks to Dorothy Pittman for her grace and intelligence, and always sage advice.

CONTENTS

12 · Contents

MANHATTAN COCKTAIL

MANHATTAN COCKTAIL: 1. Any drink or beverage used to while away the time waiting for friends to show up. 2. A blend or intoxicating mix of sophisticated urban humor.

$$\frac{\cdot}{1}\frac{}{\cdot}$$

MANHATTAN
COCKTAIL

I've been losing patience with people who make dates and habitually show up late. You know the type. In a typical scenario I'm waiting at a restaurant.

"Care for another drink?"

"No thanks, bartender, twenty-three Perriers has just about quenched my thirst, but if you'd be good enough to pass those peanuts. Thanks."

"Waiting for friends?"

"Yup."

"What time is your reservation?"

"Eight."

"It's nine thirty-five."

"I know. Hold it, I think this is them now."

"Oh, Lewis dear, we're so sorry. John had to have open heart surgery just as we were leaving the house. Hope you haven't been waiting long."

"No, of course not, just got here myself. Oh bartender, what do I owe you for the Perriers?"

"Thirty-five dollars."

Or:

"We'll pick you up at seven-thirty, okay?"

"Great."

"Mrs. Hillpuft said she'd be right down, something about a white rabbit."

"Thanks."

Radio: This is the "Rex Martin Show"

This is "Guess That Tune"

This is Lamont Cranston, The Shadow

This is "Inner Sanctum"

This is the Late News

This is Father Benjamin Mignonette

This is the 7 A.M. News, Good Morning!

"Oh, Lewis, how nice of you to wait. My dress got caught in the computer and had to be rewoven—the buttons from Paris didn't arrive until just a few minutes ago. You know how those French pilots are, as if they had all the time in the world. Why Lewis dear, you're sweating. Are you sick, do you have a fever?"

"Margaret, the party was yesterday."

"Oh dear, oh dear! I hope you're not angry."

"No, of course not. Will John be down soon?"

"Oh yes, any moment now. He was just checking the *Encyclopedia Britannica* for spelling errors."

Suppressing the urge to strangle them I foolishly play their game. If they are usually a half hour late and I want them at eight for a dinner party, I simply tell them to come at seven-thirty.

Sometimes people aren't fooled by being told to come early, especially when they have arrived early two dates running. They regroup and come an hour late the following time.

"Oh dear, are we late again?"

"No problem, Janet, the Bushes said to send you their regards. That Barbara is such a love. Maybe you can meet them next time. Care for a drink?"

Of course if you don't know the Bushes you may have to learn relaxation techniques to help you through the difficult waiting period. Personally, I would cutivate the Reagans.

Scientists have found that while waiting for a late friend to arrive, the average person experiences "contractions" or "tension spasms" of the whole body. These contractions left unattended can reduce the person waiting to a whimpering, sobbing, howling bowl of jelly. Enter Lamaze!

As the tension mounts in your upper torso and neck, and you find yourself belching hitherto unknown expletives to the bartender about your friend, begin a gentle pattern of slow, rhythmic pant-breathing accompanied by counting from one to ten. After about a half hour of this breathing, just as you are shifting into acute spasm and foaming at the mouth, try what the French call "effleurage" or butterfly stroking. Lie down across the top of the bar at the restaurant and move your fingertips in soft circles over the centers of tension (in your case your entire body). Try not to pay attention to other diners who out of ignorance may be calling an ambulance or the police. Relax!

Finally, when dealing with inveterate, degenerate late-comers, persons who flagrantly abuse your good graces and nature by asking specifically when they should meet you only so they will know when to be late—swift retribution is called for. Biblical justice.

"Hi, I hope I haven't kept you waiting long."

"Unfortunately you have, Patty." (Signalling to the executioner waiting in the wings near the brazier) "Off with her head!"

This last solution never fails to elicit responses of surprise from those who are late (pathological minds do not expect capital punishment for being late), and it really works. Unless a special presidential reprieve arrives, hand delivered, I urge you to use it. Trust me, with people like the Beemaxes it is the only way. Here they come now. Ready?

"Oh, hi dear, I hope we haven't kept you waitin'..."

"Rat-a-tat-tat-a-tat-tat-a-tat."

Others will respect you for your stand.

÷ 2 ÷

FRUMKES
FOR
PRESIDENT

I like Dukakis. Dukakis is small and cute and calls everybody "my friends," whether they are or they aren't. But we're talking about electing a president of the United States, my friends, a leader who will be the most powerful man on earth. Dukakis, with or without his friends, just isn't exciting enough. I also like George Bush. George is tall and handsome, the kind of man every divorced woman in America hopes she'll meet on a blind date. George can boogie like a demon, hit golf balls with the best of them, and model V-necked sweaters for *GQ*; but, let's face it, friends, he's just too wimpy to be president. That is why I have decided to run for president.

But where am I coming from, you ask? What is my platform? Good question.

As you probably know, the Russians are winning the arms race. Back in the seventies, when the peaceniks and mollycoddles were talking Salt II and détente, and we foolishly stopped producing arms, the devious Russians continued to build weapons behind our backs—"Build, Sergei, build! Yo, ho, heave ho! Catch the capitalist dogs now, but don't let them see you." Today they not only have parity with us, they have surpassed us in every major military area. I'm sure I don't have to tell you about their SS-20, PL-4, and PI-5 missiles, all huge and MIRVed and equipped with needles and spiders, capable of taking out planets the size of Saturn. They are awesome. Or their Gruntov Battle Titan, a gigantic evil robot that eats soldiers in the field and then spits them out again. "Ha, ha, ha! Imperialist peeg! *Grrr!* Crunch, crunch! Ha, ha, ha!" Believe me, the Russians are fiends. They are tough and mean and never show mercy. "Please, comrade, no, spare me. I will learn 'The Volga Boatmen' by heart, please—*arghhh!*" In any nuclear confrontation they would kick our teeth in. I wouldn't lie to you. If you don't want your children to be eaten by a Gruntov Battle Titan or incinerated by a nuclear missile, you had better get your priorities straight and jump on the Frumkes bandwagon now. Uncle Lew needs you!

How will I offset the Russian lead, you ask? I will build not only a Stealth bomber, that invisible flying wing you have seen drawings of in *Time* magazine, but Stealth aircraft carriers that launch invisible fighter planes, and Stealth submarines and Stealth tanks. I will build an entire Stealth army equipped with black cloaks and Reebok sneakers so that we can tiptoe across the Russian border without being detected and walk right up to Gorbachev's office inside the Kremlin walls.

"Did you hear something, Boris?" "No, not me, Mr. Chairman. It must have been the wind."

I will allow private citizens to sponsor missiles so they can really get into defense. There will be a special brass plaque on each missile, be it a Backfire, Blackjack, Pershing, or cruise, bearing your name, corporate logo, or simply "This missile is being fired in the name of Mr. and Mrs. Stuart Woevil" and your coat of arms. If the Air Force runs out of plaques before your missile is fired, your name will be handwritten in chalk on the warhead just prior to launch. Not to worry, the chalk will be a new kind that doesn't come off easily.

I will also encourage private gifts of space-age weapons to our defense establishment. Thus you will be able to channel all those profits from your Quik-Press pants business into a real Star Wars particle-beam weapon interceptor, or a high-powered, space-based infrared laser battle station. Imagine an "Etta Kirshenbaum" pop-up kinetic-energy weapons system, orbiting the earth every hour on the hour for all to see. You will also be helping your country.

These programs, jointly involving the public and private sectors, will ensure our security well into the twenty-first century.

In domestic affairs, I stand for capital punishment. While it is true that capital punishment does not discourage crimes of passion, like rape and murder, it works wonders with litterers and parking violators. Think about it, would you really double-park again if you knew for sure you would be hanged or guillotined in the town square? I thought not. Nor would you discard a gum wrapper without thinking twice:

"My God, Harry, they shot him for throwing his gum wrapper in the mailbox."

"The sonofabitch litterer!

"Harry."

The country, under Frumkes, will once again become clean and uncongested.

I also believe in participatory abortion. Under this method, a woman may have an abortion if she chooses, but the accused father will have to perform it. It will become a somewhat less attractive option.

"Whaddaya mean, I have to do the abortion? Whaddaya, crazy?"

To raise money for education, I will propose grade auctions every Sunday. A's will be $25, B's $10, C's free. True, some affluent students will become instant scholars, but that is better than doing drugs.

"Geez, will you look at this. We raised $30,000 from the 200 valedictorians. The Von Trubitz kid will deliver the commencement address."

"Can he read?"

"I don't know; he got an A for his Bugs Bunny paper last week."

Yes, my programs are bold. Yes, they are courageous.

Vote *Frumkes* on Election Day.

A vote for *Lew* is a vote for *you!*

÷
3
÷

HOW TO MAKE A FORTUNE THROUGH OSMOSIS

It isn't easy to make a fortune the old-fashioned way, no matter what you've heard. It means learning a trade or profession then slogging your way up the corporate ladder from mail room attendant, to first broom, to vice-president, and so on and so forth until you are a hundred years old. Nor is it any easier getting a bright idea and starting a business. Bright ideas by themselves are worth nothing.

"Hey Harry, what do you think of this. We take sugar cubes like the Domino sugar cubes and dress them in little suits with stars and stripes all over them and market them as "CAPTAIN SUGAR, the All-American Sweetner?" We'll make a fortune!

"Get lost Larry, I'm busy."

Second, even if the idea is brilliant like making small cars with giant rubber bumpers to reduce the danger and severity of accidents on the freeways, it is a long road between conception and making a fortune.

So why not make your fortune the easy way, by osmosis. No having to develop real estate, or drill for oil, or trade options, or raid companies—all those things you don't have the foggiest notion about. All you have to do is sidle up to a proper millionaire, according to my instructions, and presto transfuso, you will make a fortune by osmosis. Here's how.

SELECT THE TARGET

Identifying your target millionaire is the first order of business. This is complicated by the fact that many millionaires are protected by phalanxes of secretaries and yes men who guard them with their lives. "Grrrrr! Who are you? What do you want?" You will have to get your millionaire on the outside, either when he leaves the office or when he is on vacation. There he is now. He is the little gentleman sitting in the back of the stretch limousine talking through a speaker phone to his driver, Wadsworth. He is telling Wadsworth that he wants to stop for a moment at a particular shop before he goes home. It is now that you have to strike.

POSITIONING YOURSELF FOR OSMOSIS

The millionaire instructs Wadsworth to pull up in front of the boutique displaying the purple pongee polo outfit. You must move quickly. As soon as his car slows, you begin strolling in the direction of the boutique. As the millionaire walks up to the window you move in close, right next to him. You can feel the heat from his cashmere, hand-tailored jacket, and the warmth from his Fisher Island tan. He's the genuine article all right, maybe forty or fifty million. A big one. He'll never miss a small fortune. Even his accountants won't notice anything awry for a month or so. Gently, ever so gently you bring your arm in contact with his, not so he thinks you are strange or fruity, but just as if you are another interested party, a man of similar tastes and breeding, who is also into purple polo outfits. There, you can feel it now, the sudden surge of power as hundreds of thousands of dollars course between the millionaire and yourself. It is a heady experience and for a moment you may feel flushed as if you have earned it all yourself. Not to worry. You have not. You are still the same person you were, only richer as the moments go by. When you think you have reached your goal, in this case a modest to large fortune, disengage yourself from the millionaire just as smoothly and discreetly as you began and move toward the curb. You will find a car and driver waiting for you now, your own car. Not as large or fine as the millionaire's car—maybe it's a Mercedes and he has a Rolls, but a car and driver nevertheless befitting your new station in life. Get in and say, "Home Mike." Perhaps when you run your stake into tens of millions, you can have a driver named Charles or Barcroft, but for now it's Mike.

In the second instance you spot your millionaire while he is on vacation. Though your accommodations may be quite different—he has a penthouse suite, you have a modest single overlooking the parking lot—there are places at the Caribbeana you have in common: the Rendezvous bar, for example, the one by the pool with the thatched roof and the fantastic piña coladas. It is five in the afternoon and the millionaire has left his yacht and is sitting at the bar with his two well-groomed blondes in attendance. Fortunately, the blondes are both parked to his left. You take the seat to his right and order a yellow-bird. His ears perk up at the mention of a yellow-bird. He wonders what a yellow-bird is. Why doesn't he know about it? When the drink arrives the millionaire looks up.

"Excuse me," he says, "but what is a yellow-bird?"

"Try it," you say, "it's pineapple juice and twelve different kinds of exotic rums."

You proffer your drink, as if to say, "Here, taste, don't be frightened." Skeptical at first, the millionaire finally succumbs to curiosity and reaches for the drink. It is at this moment that osmosis takes over. As the millionaire's lips touch the glass and he drains some golden liquid from it, large blocks of stock from both the New York and American exchanges somehow are transferred into the glass and find their way to your account at Shearson American Express. They are not even on margin. When you return home you will be greeted with new respect by your broker. But for now it will suffice that your room has been changed to ocean view, 12, and that an attractive brunette at the end of the bar is batting her eyes at you.

Making a fortune through osmosis is as easy as that once you know what you are doing. And now that you have the hang of it, you can meet millionaires at the race track, on vacation, in fancy restaurants, and at the club. In fact that is why most people on their way up join clubs, so they can sidle up to other millionaires and continue to augment their fortunes. It is the American way.

$$\div 4 \div$$

THE JOYS
OF BALDING

There it is, just barely visible in the mirror as I rotate my head all the way to the left and look over my shoulder—exactly where Amber said it was, though she mistakenly described it as "the size of North Dakota." Actually, it is only a little patch of skin, more like Rhode Island or Aruba, in the back, where probably no one will notice. Maybe I can cover it over with my hair, or darken it with some stain.

"Damn! I'm going bald!"

"What did you say, Dad?"

"Oh, hi, honey. I didn't realize you were still standing here. Is school out?"

"Looking at your bald spot, Dad?"

"Well, not exactly, honey, just kind of seeing where my part..."

"Mr. Cooper's bald from ear to ear, Dad, even worse than you."

"I, I, ..."

"You could comb your hair over it, Dad, maybe if you parted your hair on the other side...."

"Look, Amber, I really don't want to talk about my hair, okay?"

"Touchy, touchy, Dad."

But there's no use pretending any more. It's there, along with the almost imperceptible stoop in my posture that has occurred in the last few years.

"Dad, you're all hunched over. And you're bald. You look like Quasimodo. Why don't you stand up straight?"

"Amber, don't you have any homework?"

"I did it all in school, Dad."

Fortunately, there are subtle ways to disguise this almost invisible effect of incipient hair loss. I am certain no one at the club will even give a second glance.

"Lew baby! Why are you wearing a hat to the club? Got a bald spot?"

"No, Harvey, my wife gave me this hat as a gift."

"Sure she did Lew. But we're in the sauna bath in the men's locker room. It's 220 degrees. Hey, being bald isn't so bad."

"I said, 'I'm not bald,' Harvey."

"No you didn't, Lew. You said your wife gave you the hat as a gift. Touchy, touchy!"

"Goofonzola cagutz!" (This old Aramaic expression may loosely be translated as, "Your mother came out of a seed.")

I confess, the thought of going bald was beginning to depress me. I was becoming obsessed with baldness. I looked up "bald" in the dictionary when nobody was looking. The dictionary said, "1. lacking hair on the scalp: a bald head; a bald person. (so cruel) 2. destitute of some natural growth or covering (moi?): a bald mountain. 3. lacking detail or vividness; plain (me plain?): a bald prose style (now they were attacking my writing) 4. open or forthright; undisguised (that's fair, I am these things): a bald lie. 5. having white on the head (no question about it): the bald eagle.

Scary questions sprang to mind. How bald would I ultimately become? Would I resemble Yul Brynner or King

Kong Bundy? Would people take me for a skinhead, a large billiard ball, or a tumor? Would my virility disappear with my hair? Would women start to pass me by and forsake me for younger men, or at least, younger appearing men? This terrifying thought caused me to wake up nights in a cold sweat looking for hair on my pillow. Eventually, I would cry myself back to sleep. I became so disconsolate that I took up the dictionary again and started to look up words like "ball." 1. a spherical or approximately spherical body (my God, they know that too); I didn't want to hear any more. Amber tried to comfort me.

"Don't worry, Dad, hair isn't everything. You've still got a long nose."

"Don't you have homework, Amber?"

"Dad, why don't you think of it this way. When you do competitive swimming, you will have less water resistance than the other people, no drag. All the male swimmers at school shave their heads."

"Amber, honey, why don't you call your friend Magpie and see what she's doing today?"

"Touchy, touchy, aren't we?"

Snake oil salesmen entered my life in a big way. Where hitherto I had laughed along with everyone else at their ridiculous claims, I now took them seriously. Suddenly, it seemed plausible that Dr. Zeus's hair cream made from dragon's breath and the ground horns of unborn rhinoceroses would somehow stimulate my scalp to produce follicles. I bought every hair cream on the market and smeared and lathered my head with the hope of growing new locks.

At the club I took a curious interest in exotic hair tonics and wondered what would happen if I drank the blue liquid in the comb tank. To no avail. I read books on hair health, massaged my pate regularly, said mantras, and prayed to "Breck" the Egyptian god of hair. Nothing.

Finally, in desperation, I decided to adopt a positive attitude. To accept the inevitable. (Why had this not occurred to me before?) There were indeed certain joys of balding. As time went by, I discovered the following:

1. Bald men do not have to produce an ID in a bar when they want a drink.
2. Bald men do not get dandruff.
3. Bald men can make extra money selling space on their heads to advertisers.
4. Once bald, you no longer have to fear going bald.
5. Baldness is not without its appeal. Think of it this way. Wouldn't you rather eat a smooth hard-boiled egg than a hard-boiled egg that has hair all over it? Be honest!
6. Amber was right. There *is* less resistance when you swim.
7. Bald is clean. (Remember Mr. Clean?)
8. Bald people project machismo and virility. (Telly Savalas, Gorbachev, Marvelous Marvin Hagler.)
9. A bald head requires little in the way of upkeep (a little polish once in a while).
10. Bald is beautiful.

Soon I became proud of my baldness, no longer bothering to hide it. I displayed it with pride at every turn and even flaunted it. I took pleasure in out-performing my younger looking rivals in golf, tennis, and swimming. And when an attractive-looking filly came on to me at the first tee one day over some of those younger, long-haired, male members, I knew she suspected what every bald man knows but keeps to himself, "a bald head means a very large . . . bank book."

$$\frac{\vdots}{5}$$

FUTURE BEST-SELLERS

In a reversal of policy, we have decided to review books before they are written rather than after, thus saving authors who receive poor notices two or three years of wasted effort writing the books. Most writers have been supportive of this new policy and have encouraged us to review their books while still in the embryonic thought stage.

The following books will become best-sellers in the near future and are being written even as you read this.

FICTION

Rabbit Rest, by John Updike (Knopf, $12.95). Rabbit Angstrom of *Rabbit Run, Rabbit Redux, Rabbit Is Rich, Rabbit Redoubtable, Rabbit Roué,* and *Rabbit Repentant* is back again in *Rabbit Rest,* the concluding volume of Updike's peculiar septuplet. This time Harry runs out of pellets.

The Ottoman Empire, by Harold Robbins (Simon and Schuster, $13.95). Robbins's disquieting roman à clef about the upholstery industry is a veritable "who stuffs whom" set among the antimacassars of Rome, Paris, and Istanbul.

Stupidos, by Stephen King (Viking, $13.95). The story of an inept New England family in the 70 percent bracket who have never heard of tax shelters. Full of fiery and recriminatory "You should have"s and "I told you so"s.

Nibble House, by James Clavell (Delacorte, $19.95). British and Chinese businessmen struggle for control of one of Hong Kong's oldest fried noodle companies. Financial crunch.

Homburg Heaven, by Martin Cruz Smith (Random House, $13.95). A multiple murder in London leads Henderson of Scotland Yard through the millinery underground of Europe and Central America to "Mr. Big," a Mexican sombrero, size 12XXXXX.

The Puppets of God, by Morris West (Morrow, $14.95). What happens when an observant journalist notices strings attached to the Pope and all his cardinals in Rome? Where do they lead? Why do the prelates of St. Peter's secretly dance around like dervishes, hardly making contact with the floor? And where does that music come from? Spooky.

The Hotel Igloo, by John Irving (Dutton, $15.50). Life with the Clauses, a strange red-suited family who set up house in the North Pole with their reindeer and elves. Bizarre wrestling scenes.

NONFICTION

The Middle East Diet, by Judy Mazel with Sheik Yamani (Macmillan, $10.95). A low-calorie, high-octane diet that depends for its success on personal motivation and good spark plugs. A variation of the highly acclaimed Saudi Arabian Diet.

You Can Talk Anybody into Anything, by Herb Cohen (Lyle Stuart, $12.95). The secret: You get more with a smile and a .45 than with just a smile.

The One-Minute Lover, by Jack Whisk (Doubleday, $14.95). Case histories of fabulous quick lovers from Trigger McGhee to Pistol Pete Foxglove. Author tackles premature ejaculation and the controversial use of starting guns. Not for those with yearning disabilities.

AND BEAR IN MIND . . .

The Stories of Idi Amin (Farrar, Straus & Giroux, $17.95). Twenty-five stories from 1968 to the present, chosen by the author and told in "gibberish," his native tongue. Always amusing, occasionally lucid.

$$\frac{\dot{}}{6}$$
$$\dot{}$$

SUING
SANTA
<u>CLAUS</u>

I hope this doesn't become popular, because that could mean tens of millions of copycat law suits, ad nauseum, as greedy malcontents jump on the litigation bandwagon, but the Frumkes family has begun an action against Santa Claus, aka Kris Kringle, aka St. Nicholas, aka Father Christmas, aka Père Noel, in the Supreme Court of the State of New York. As it now appears, the suit grew out of the disappointing response by Santa Claus to the repeated letters (See schedule A attached, exhibits A,B,C, and D) from the Frumkes children asking for certain appropriate and deserved gifts which he apparently had promised if they were good, and to which they felt they were entitled.

SCHEDULE A, EXHIBITS A,B,C, & D

Decembers 5, 1985, '86, '87, & '88

Dear Santa,

My sister, Rapunzel, and I have been good all year and you promised that if we were, you would bring us whatever we want. Here are the toys we want, Santa:

A. An exploding football—the kind that goes off when it is either kicked or caught. I think they make them in Taiwan or Libya, Santa.
B. The new "Action" Barbie doll, Santa. You know the one—she comes with see-through undies, a diaphragm, and two disposable Kens.
C. 4 large blobs of "Stupid Putty." This is the old-fashioned kind, Santa, that bounces when you drop it, and can be used effectively to caulk your nose when you have a cold.
D. A Rambo "Trap the Commie and Step on His Face" board game.

Sincerely,

Sultan Frumkes

Neither in 1985, '86, '87, or '88, did Santa Claus provide said gifts which the kids alleged he had promised, but left instead some educational toys, clothing, and books which the children felt were neither in keeping with the holiday spirit or their expectations. "Get real, Dad." In their affidavit the children also maintained that they were not spoiled or over-reaching in their requests and that Santa had led them to believe that the gifts requested would be forthcoming.

The Frumkes family is also participating in a class action suit brought by the tenants of 619 East 82nd Street against this same Santa Claus. It alleges that on the night of December 24th sometime between the hours of 10 P.M. and 5 A.M. the following morning, said Santa Claus did land on the roof of 619 East 82nd street with eight tiny reindeer called respectively: Dasher, Dancer, Prancer, Vixen, Comet, Cupid, Donner, and Blitzen, and possibly a ninth with a luminous nose called Doowop, or something which sounded like that, and did cause injury to the roof tiles, parapet walls, and plantings of 619 East 82nd Street in the act of landing as well as leave droppings over the entire roof area without respect to either the privacy or ownership of said roof of said building.

It is further alleged that on this night of December 24th, between the hours of 10 P.M. and 5 A.M. the following morning, this same Santa Claus without permission did break into and enter some one hundred twenty apartments of 619 East 82nd Street, which constitutes all apartments at that address, and variously left toys, trinkets, and food stuffs of unknown origin in living rooms and foyer areas without regard to tenant privacy or appointments. In several apartments he raised such a ruckus and clatter that a number of the children and their parents did awaken from their sleep to see what was the matter.

The action also states that the party known as Santa Claus, aka Kris Kringle, aka St. Nicholas, aka Father Christmas, aka Père Noel is neither related to any of the tenants or personally known to them and as such had no business being on their building at such an inauspicious and questionable hour of the night, especially landing on the roof in the company of some dozen animals and then proceeding down the building's chimney with care into the respective tenants' apartments.

In the class action the tenants are seeking one million dollars in punitive damages from Mr. Claus and the understanding that he will not return to 619 East 82nd Street at any time in the future unbidden, unless he wants his ass shot off. If this is agreed upon and acceded to they will not at this time press criminal charges against Mr. Claus, though they reserve that right should he land on their building again anytime in the future.

As far as the Frumkeses are concerned, they are not seeking any punitive measures against Mr. Claus, but rather a binding order from the court that he fulfill his promises to the children for the years 1985, '86, '87, and '88.

Author's note:

Both suits were settled amicably out of court earlier this month.

FACT SHEET ON METER MAIDS

WHAT ARE METER MAIDS?

Meter maids are invisible pests that ticket your car, usually for the maximum forty dollars, the moment you leave it double-parked. They are ubiquitous and specially bred by the Department of Motor Vehicles to show no mercy.

WHERE DO THEY COME FROM?

No one knows for sure. Some theorists speculate that the first meter maid may have occurred when a drunken KGB agent, lonely beyond belief, accidentally mated with a large North American Termite in the dark woods near the U.S.–Canadian border.

WHAT DO THEY LOOK LIKE?

It has been reported that meter maids are ugly, and bear a red hourglass configuration on their backs. They apparently wear drab brown uniforms with which they try to emulate real police officers. If you should see one it would be wise to beat a hasty retreat.

IS THERE ANY WAY TO WARD THEM OFF?

Some motorists feel that cloves of garlic loosely draped across the hood of the car will keep the meter maids away, while others use silver bullets and stakes through the heart to discourage them. A group known as the Meter Maid Busters has gone so far as to market Meter Maid Motels in highly trafficked areas, which are liberally laced with meter maid poison.

HOW MANY METER MAIDS ARE THERE?

While the precise number has not been determined, there are thought to be several million in New York City alone. There is not a street or avenue in Manhattan, for example, that is not surveilled by a minimum of a hundred of the dread creatures, day and night. In fact, the dark clouds that occasionally roll over this great city are thought by meteorologists to be nothing more than meter maids changing guard.

DO METER MAIDS HAVE INTELLIGENCE?

This is a moot question. Until recently it was thought that meter maids operated solely on instinct, like homing pigeons or torpedoes, and possessed no real intelligence in the sense that humans do. But some researchers now believe that meter maids may possess some rudimentary intelligence after all, though not enough where it would do you any good to argue with them.

HAS THERE BEEN ANY ATTEMPT BY THE FEDERAL GOVERNMENT TO REGULATE THE PRODUCTION OF METER MAIDS?

In 1984 a bill was introduced by certain farsighted individuals in the House of Representatives to have the firstborn child of each meter maid fixed, but it was quickly defeated on the floor by pro-life liberals.

IS IT TRUE THAT METER MAIDS ARE PROLIFERATING AT A GEOMETRIC RATE AND THAT BY THE YEAR 2000 THE PLANET WILL BE CHOKED BY THEM?

Yes.

IS THERE ANYTHING WE CAN DO AT ALL TO STEM THE TIDE?

At the present time, I'm afraid not.

THIS

SEMESTER

AT

FRUMKES U.

DRESSING FOR SUCCESS #336

Creating the right image whether for business or social reasons is very important in today's competitive society. Learn what it takes to create a successful image from one of America's most distinguished climbers: how he made it in the fabled "Hamptons." Learn to economize by only dressing your front; why bondage pants and combat boots are no longer considered "chic" among Palm Beach socialites and old dowagers; what kind of person believes "them as has 'em wears 'em."

Classes meet Tuesday and Thursday evenings 7 P.M. at Bloomingdale's. Students are required to furnish their own "threads."

MEL PUKSTERN—holds a BFA in "Dressing Up" from the Fashion Institute of Technology and is fashion consultant to several chain store presidents.

MIDLIFE CRISIS   #346

How to tell when you are entering it; having it; leaving it. Discussion of symptoms: i.e., trying to flush yourself down the toilet; servicing the New York Football Giants if you are a woman or inviting Sweet Briar College to your apartment for a long weekend if you are a man; painting your hair in Day-Glo colors. Remedies: i.e., trying to flush yourself down the toilet; servicing the New York Football Giants if you are a woman or inviting Sweet Briar College to your apartment for a long weekend if you are a man; painting your hair in Day-Glo colors.

Wednesday evenings 6–10 P.M.

MRS RENÉ HENRY McKNIGHT WILLIAMS SCHWARTZ BARBARINI HAZEN-QUILL—is the author of *My Way* and a real life survivor of the midlife crisis.

HIP HYPNOSIS   #370

Hypnosis is a safe, effective skill that you can learn to improve your life and the lives of others. It has been successfully used to help people lose weight, stop smoking, and stand in front of a large audience imitating a jack rabbit.

During the semester students will study various techniques of inducing hypnosis, including the classic "sleep, sleep" and "thwomp" over the head with a club which has recently been declared illegal in several states.

The term ends with a secret posthypnotic suggestion which is really not a secret any more now that the students have taken the course seventeen times running.

Thursdays at noon.

THE GREAT CALIBAN—is staff hypnotist and feed conductor at the Bronx Zoo. He also maintains a private practice in New York.

POW, ZIF, BAM—ORIENTAL ASSERTIVENESS TRAINING #381

Standing up for your rights and communicating these needs are important to your self-esteem and self-respect.

No more allowing yourself to be chosen as effigy at the club voodoo night; backed down by your grandmother in a fight over who sits where at the dinner table; having to pay protection money to your children.

Students will learn forty different ways of saying "no"—nyet, nope, negative, nix, na na na, to name a few. Each has a killer move to back it up. Life becomes a bowl of cherries as you read the work of Niccolò Machiavelli, Idi Amin, and Zorba the Greek and learn to get what you want through the ancient art of Pow, Zif, Bam.

Method acting helps you identify with tanks, tractors, ploughs, and other things that get where they are going; helps you master the art. No more giving in, mollycoddling, acquiescing—next time it's Pow, Zif, Bam.

Fridays 4–6 P.M.

DR. ROCK CHOW—is a plaid belt, twentieth don, Pow, Zif, Bam master who punches even before he thinks. Lightning fast, he was used as an explosive during the Vietnam War.

INTELLIGENCE 101—WORKSHOP   #387

I–101 is a comprehensive course which will examine theory as well as practical aspects of intelligence getting. Students will study numerous intelligence societies; i.e., Mensa, 4–Sigma, One-in-a-Thousand, Big Brain, etc., as well as methods of increasing the I.Q.: such as eating gifted children; lying; taking vitamin C; squeezing the head.

As your intelligence increases you will find less and less reason to take the course until finally you will drop out. In fact, we have been so successful in the past that most students leave I–101 wondering why they ever took it in the first place.

Classes meet all day Sunday.

CECIL (THE MEDULLA) THORNHILL—I.Q. 203 and growing.

AUTO-GRAFFITI   #392

Auto-Graffiti, the art of decorating yourself, is one of the most popular classes at Frumkes U. You will learn how to work with a mirror, helper, back-swab, and reflectobrush; explore the myriad catch-phrases and names used in classic graffiti, including—"Satan," "Kilroy Was Here," and "Melinda Hot-Lips 924–7783," as well as a few that transcend the traditional vocabulary such as, "_ _ _ _," and the much beloved "_ _ _ _ _ _ _."

Students will experiment with lipstick, watercolor, egg tempera, and colored yogurts before deciding on the medium in which they want to work.

Classes meet midnight to 2 A.M.—locations to be announced.

RALPH—is a member of the Billboard School and studied with the legendary "Stingo."

÷9÷

TWENTY-THOUSAND LEAGUES UNDER THE SINK

Recently a 54-year-old southern author who attended Vassar College on a scholarship from the United Daughters of the Confederacy was chosen to write a sequel to *Gone With The Wind*. This in turn has spawned a rash of sequels to classic and contemporary literary works, as publishers rush to cash in on the masters. Among the exciting new titles on the horizon are:

THE CANOEIAD

A sequel to The Iliad in which Telemachus, the son of Odysseus, who is not too bright, sets out in a canoe to recapture Troy from his own people. Since the journey requires traveling 99 percent over land by canoe, Telemachus has difficulty recruiting able seamen to join him on the "Canoeiad," and must go it alone. When Telemachus inadvertently paddles into a tree and destroys his canoe, the whole mission is aborted and Telemachus returns home to Penelope who suggests that maybe he should go into therapy.

ROMEO AND HARRIET

Apparently sly Romeo was only faking his suicide as a star-crossed lover in the original play and had drunk a cup of decaffeinated coffee instead of a cup of poison. The sequel finds Romeo sneaking out of the tomb at night to meet Harriet Capulet, Juliet's older sister (Shakespeare was unaware of her existence), whom Romeo has secretly loved all along. His problem had been how to get rid of Juliet. Harriet and Romeo run off together to live in another town but are discovered by Benvolio who becomes very disturbed when he sees them. Romeo tries to explain that it was too bad about Juliet and Tybalt and Mercutio, and how he regrets what happened, but Benvolio will have none of it. Benvolio then utters the immortal words, "Romeo, you #@#*@!, you are dead meat." The sequel ends with Romeo and Harriet running for their lives through the hills of Verona while Benvolio chases them with an ax.

THE GREATEST GATSBY

After the death of Jay Gatsby, his youngest son, Donald, who has an ego problem, arrives on the scene to claim his inheritance. Donald Gatsby sells his father's fabulous estate in West Egg for eighteen billion dollars and uses the proceeds to develop real estate in New York City. He calls his projects Gatsby Tower, Gatsby Plaza, Gatsby Castle, etc., in a gentle effort to assert his own strong personality. After buying Mar-A-Lago in Palm Beach, Adnan Khashoggi's yacht, and the Plaza Hotel, Donald continues to close deal after deal until he owns the entire world.

TWENTY-THOUSAND LEAGUES UNDER THE SINK

A giant sea serpent is reported loose under the sink of M. Kessler on East 72nd St. Immediately an investigative party is dispatched by the Department of Health to get to the bottom of the mystery. Included in the party are one Professor Aronnax, a teacher of writing in the lifelong learning center of Marymount Manhattan College, several netters, and Ed Land, a harpoonist and developer of the Polaroid Land Camera. The serpent, curiously enough, turns out to be only an errant atomic submarine commanded by a Captain Nemo which somehow made a wrong turn at New London, Connecticut. After reporting his findings back to the Department of Health, Professor Aronnax is placed in a garbage compactor and terminated.

CYRANO RETROUSSÉ

In *Cyrano Retroussé*, Cyrano de Bergerac has returned from the dead and married his cousin Roxanne. He has had his nose bobbed by one of the best rhinoplasts in New York and works in the junk bond department of Drexel Burnham Lambert. Cyrano and Roxanne have two funny-looking children with trunks and severe learning disabilities. Tutors come to the house day and night. Despite these minor problems, the couple is very happy. The trouble starts when the de Bergeracs are at a theatre benefit for the kids' school and another parent makes some remarks about Cyrano's button-cute nose.

FRANKENSTEIN II

In the original version Victor Frankenstein's monster fled across the ice field at the end of the novel and froze to death. In the sequel we find that he was actually preserved intact until 1989 when a suburban skater, mistaking him for her husband, tries to hack him to death, thereby releasing him. The monster then makes his way to the big city where he is immediately recognized as Alfred Lord Tennyson, Poet Laureate of England, and offered a position as assistant in the mail room of Harrods. At Harrods he falls in love with Dhroomy, a giant panda who has escaped from the London Zoo and is shopping for an art deco sculpture. Dhroomy's keeper finds the monster making love to Dhroomy in the stationery department, of all places, and shoots him through the heart. As he lays dying, the monster looks up at the keeper and asks the haunting question, "What are you, crazy or something?"

CANDUDE

A contemporary sequel to Voltaire's satire, Candide has wised up, come out of the garden, and become "Candude," a major stud.

"How's it goin' man?"
"Slip me five, baby!"

Announcing that New York is the best of all possible cities, Candude sets out uptown in search of drugs. After easily making contact with dozens of pushers and purchasing his fill of coke and crack, he arrests the pushers and reads them their rights. You guessed it, he is really Sergeant Candude, Narcotics.

10

NOW IS
A GOOD TIME
TO PLANT
BULBS

Now is as good a time as any to plant electric bulbs. Since electric bulbs do not flower the same way tulip bulbs or hyacinths do, there is no need to be concerned about the season. That is the beauty of electric bulbs; they are virtually season-proof.

My fondness for bulbs, those marvelous storehouses of potential electric energy and luminosity, traces back to my childhood when my uncle first gave me a bulb, and I chose to plant it in the garden in back of our house. While other bulbs rotted in the ground or sprang into blossom in the Spring only to wilt a few weeks later, my bulbs stayed pristine and pearly, season after season, bewildering the rabbits and birds who broke their teeth on them. I loved the way they looked in the garden, like little white spheroid mushrooms, or eggs in a nest, perfectly symmetrical, glistening in the sun. Nor has my interest in bulb planting diminished over the years. On any bright morning you can find me hard at work in my garden, screwing bulbs into the ground with the same enthusiasm and excitement that caused me to take up bulb-planting as a hobby thirty years ago.

HOW TO BUY BULBS

When you buy bulbs be sure to deal with reputable hardware stores or 5 & 10's. Wrapped in their little cardboard boxes, bulbs can hide, even from a practiced eye, subtle internal damages and manufacturing defects that can cause them to explode in the ground. No one wants to go through the agony of planting bulbs in intricate and delicate geometric patterns in the garden only to then have to say:

"Shit! My bulbs exploded,"
and be left to pick up all the little glass fragments and cutting your hands to ribbons before finally replacing them.

Also, the terminology under which bulbs are sold can be confusing. Some are classified by their circumference in feet or inches: such as, "two-footer," or "1½ incher," while others are graded by their candle power, "2500 cpw," or wattage, "100 watts," "250 watts," etc.

It would be better for planting purposes if they were just labeled "jumbo" or "weenie," the way most people refer to them. But, alas, that is not the case, and the packages are still labeling them for the lamp-buyers and electricians rather than the "bulbers."

In short, whenever you are buying bulbs in earnest and not just fondling them in a garage or utility closet, you can tell the good ones from the bad ones by picking them up. Healthy bulbs are firm and have no soft spots, bruises, or blemishes, and they don't rattle when you shake them.

HOW TO PLANT BULBS

True bulbs such as 100 watters, 3-ways, and little Zampa candelabra bulbs can be screwed into the soil until their brass bases and ring contacts are covered, then jostled around until they stand straight.

Fluorescent bulbs require somewhat different handling. Generally, they are laid in rows, usually six or eight inches apart and held in place with "U" clamps which are fastened to each end and stuck into the ground.

Giant klieg light bulbs and floods are planted much the same as true bulbs, though they require a larger area unto themselves. If you have never planted a klieg light bulb before, the show bulbs of any garden, you are in for a special treat.

FORCING BULBS

Generally, I force bulbs into the soil with brute strength trying not to put too much pressure on the top of the bulb so as to break it. I also wear thick gloves when forcing bulbs so I don't lacerate myself too badly when a bulb does shatter, as they are bound to do now and then. For really intransigent bulbs I like to put my foot on top of them and gradually apply my weight until they sink into the soil with a little wimper. Occasionally, though, I get carried away and jump up and down on them, cursing,

   "Get in there, goddamit!"

But I recommend the slow and patient approach in the beginning.

BULB LORE

Electric bulbs have been around ever since Thomas Edison first blew one out of glass in the early part of the 20th century, naïvely expecting that it would be used exclusively for producing light. Edison was a great inventor but lacked vision; he never imagined how attractive bulbs would look planted in the ground.

   In 1933, the German horticulturist Wilhelm Dreschnitz planted a bulb in his backyard quite by accident and was amazed how good it looked. Soon friends of his emulated his techniques and "bulbing," as the planting of electric bulbs is called, was on.

   For me personally, planting electric bulbs has grown into more than just a hobby; it has become an obsession, and I plant my bulbs twenty-four hours a day, 365 days a year. I don't necessarily assume that everyone else will share my love of "bulbing" to the same degree, but I hope they will.

$$\frac{\bullet}{\bullet}$$

11

PALMING
A
BOEING 747

Palming a Boeing 747 is not half as difficult as it may seem at first glance, and it is a spectacular effect when you produce the plane out of thin air. The secret is to cover the wings and tail assembly which tend to stick out two or three hundred feet from either side of your hand. Once this is mastered you will be able to palm the 747 as easily as any other object. However, it will take a great deal of practice. Even George

Schindler, who has big hands, had to practice for several years before he could palm a 747.

Begin by palming small engine planes, Piper Cubs and Cherokees, working your way up to Lear jets, then DC–9s, and finally 747s. In time you will acquire the technique.

Also, patter is important to distract the audience. I usually try something like the following:

"Welcome aboard your Boeing 747 jumbo jet aircraft, ladies and gentlemen. This afternoon we will be showing, *Tarzan Meets the Pygmy Wart Hogs* for your entertainment."

While they are watching the movie, I pick up the plane by the tail and palm it in my left hand taking care to cover the wings and tail assembly. Since the lights are turned down low for the movie, the audience rarely sees me do this.

Immediately following the movie and before their eyes have had a chance to adjust, I do a few flourishes in the air with my left hand and produce the 747 to audible gasps.

Believe me, it is one hell of a trick.

$$\frac{\bullet}{12}$$
$$\overline{}$$

FEELINGS
OF
REJECTION

Few people are aware that like many of us, Sigmund Freud, the father of psychoanalysis, went through a major career crisis in midlife during which time he seriously considered becoming a magazine journalist. From what historians have been able to reconstruct, Freud apparently submitted article after article to the major periodicals of his time only to be met with the most common of all responses, rejection. At first Freud took the rejection with good spirit and determination, and like all beginning writers, continued on and persevered. But soon he grew angry and rancorous at the little slips which seemed to come in the mail every day and he began making obscene phone calls to editors and leaving bombs on their doorsteps. Friends and family concerned about this bitterness and unseemly behavior sought to cool Freud down and restore his good sense the only way they knew how—by putting his testicles in a wine press and trying to make Beaujolais. One can only surmise from the following letters released last week by the Freud Archives that had Freud encountered more success in his neophyte writing endeavors instead of rejection, the world might have lost one of its great psychological pioneers. On the other hand, had Freud got lucky, and sold one of his pieces, to *Penthouse*, say—he, not I, might have been writing this essay now. Whew!

Dear Professor Freud,

We enjoyed reading your dreams, especially the one where you are transformed against your will into a vibrator in the Rockettes' dressing room. Editors here found the accompanying illustrations most graphic and imaginative. Have you thought about getting some help? It may not be too late.

Yours Sincerely,

Otto Von Runtz
Psychology Today

Dear Dr. Freud,

Your article proclaiming that Babe Ruth used his "big bat" to compensate for his humiliating drag name and wouldn't have hit as well otherwise, is certainly original, but not the sort of thing we do here at *Sports Illustrated*. We are not into mocking great baseball heroes. And while we are at it, what kind of name is "Sigmund?" Sounds a little suspicious if you ask me. Get lost Sigmund. Take a walk!

Matt Gronk
Sports Illustrated

Dear Dr. Freud,

Personally, I found your piece on penis envy fascinating, but it is not really the type of thing we publish in *House Beautiful*. I have enclosed some back issues for you to study.

Getting back to 'WOW! DID YOU SEE THAT?', perhaps you might try *Playgirl* or *Cosmo*. In any event, thanks for letting us take a look at it if you know what I mean.

Sincerely,

Priscilla Flowerbottom
House Beautiful Magazine

Dear Dr. Freud,

Thank you for submitting your review of *Cyrano de Bergerac* to the *New York Times*'s Arts & Leisure section. While your interpretation of the play, that of Cyrano as a latent homosexual who frightens people with his phallic nose and has yet to work through his oedipal conflicts, is novel, it does, we feel, rather effectively kill the play's romantic qualities.

On behalf of the few romantics left these days, "STUFF IT!"

De Guiche
Arts & Leisure

Dear Dr. Freud,

Thank you for sending us your article, "I Am Joe's Penis." Unfortunately, we do not find it suitable for *Reader's Digest* since fifty percent of our readers do not have one. Remember, we are a general audience magazine that must appeal to all segments of the population. Have you tried *Popular Mechanics?*

Yours,

Rebecca Shoe
Reader's Digest

Dear Dr. Freud,

I'm afraid your humorous piece "Psychopathology of Everyday Life" didn't meet with much enthusiasm here, especially that part about Grenzfragen des Nerven-und Seelenlebens, which has been done to death.

Sorry.

C. Jung
Scientific American

Dear Dr. Freud,

No, we did not make a slip—this is not *NEW DORK MAGAZINE* and we are not interested in your article, "10," which rates the best hung studs in this area.

Cordially,

Jack Strap
New York Magazine

Dear Dr. Freud,

Thank you for submitting "Exploring the Unconscious" and the accompanying map of your psyche to *National Geographic*. Until June, however, we will be concentrating on terrestrial stories and known territories. Have you tried *Starwind* or *Omni?*

Sincerely,

C. Van Allen
National Geographic

Dear Dr. Freud,

We appreciate the offer to share your patient list with *The Star*. As you suggested it contains many "surprises" and "juicy tidbits." Unfortunately, one of the "juicy tidbits" owns a controlling interest in *The Star* and other important enterprises crosta-globa. If I were you I'd get out of town fast.

The Editor
The Star

TRUTHTELLERS

AND

LIARS

Do you remember the old truthteller-liar problems where there was this island on which there were only truthtellers and liars—and truthtellers always told the truth, and liars always told the opposite—and how you came across three natives but didn't know which they were? So you asked the first one which he was, to clear things up, and he mumbled something you couldn't understand. Then you turned to the second native and asked what the first one had said, and he replied evasively, "The first one said he was a liar." And you knew there was something fishy about this second one, but you couldn't quite put your finger on it. So you turned to the third native who had just been standing there quietly saying nothing, and you asked him about the first one, to which he replied, "The first one said he was a truthteller." And there was something in this third one's eye when he said it that made you want to believe him. Nevertheless, it was not proof enough. It was only a hunch and you needed more.

Fortunately, you remembered your lessons from Logic 101 and proceeded to reason thusly: What would number One have answered if he were a liar?

Answer: He would have said, "I'm a truthteller."

Good! Now what would he have said if he were a truthteller?

Answer: He would have said, "I'm a truthteller."

Aha! No matter what number One was, he would have had to answer he was a truthteller. Yet number Two had said that number One had said he was a liar. Therefore, ipso facto, number Two must be the liar and number Three the truthteller.

Bravo! You have found out what number Two and number Three are. They are the liar and the truthteller respectively. But something has been rankling you, eating away at you, inexorably and metaphysically, all these years, and you've never quite been able to understand it.

At first, you thought it was your wife—that she was getting on your nerves with her hostile little questions about where you went on Saturday nights and who the little floozy was she heard you went to the opera with. So you shed your wife in a quickie Mexican divorce and moved in with the little floozy from the opera. But soon the floozy began to get on your nerves, too, with her theatrical way of marching around the apartment like a Prussian soldier, goosestepping, and constantly summoning you to her side with "Indian Love Call."

Then you moved out finally realizing that it was something more fundamental that was tormenting you. Now you went to an analyst and spent twenty years sorting out your family until you could easily tell your mother from your father (your mother is the one with the rolling pin, your father has the club). But still you cannot relieve the incessant itch that is driving you crazy.

And then one day you know what it is. You have never satisfactorily resolved the question, "What was number One?" True, you have found out about number Two and number Three—that they were a liar and a truthteller, but who cares? It is number One you really want to know about. The one who mumbled something under his breath. What did he really say all those years ago? What was he? What was number One? What was number One?

You call your travel agent immediately and ask to revisit the island of truthtellers and liars. He makes the necessary arrangements and sends you on your way. There it is, just as you remember it, vague and nebulous. And you are not there two minutes when you encounter three natives, the same three who greeted you lo those many years ago. Only now the three natives are slightly stooped and number One is losing his hair.

"What are you?" you ask number One. And he smiles like the cat who has just swallowed the canary and mumbles something you can't hear. So number Two says, "He said he was a liar." Only this time you don't just stand there like a dummy waiting for number Three to add, "He said he was a truthteller." Instead, you leap at number One, grab him by the throat, and start to pummel his head shouting, "What are you? What are you, you sonofabitch? Tell me right now or I'll kill you, so help me God!"

And number One gasps, "Let me go! I'll tell you. What are you crazy or something? Okay, Okay. I'm a liar."

"But how do I know you're a liar?" you say, tightening your grip on his throat.

"What would I have said if I were a liar?" he rasps, barely getting the words out.

"You would have said you were a truthteller," you reply.

"Right! Right!" he gasps. "And what would I say if I was a truthteller?"

"You would say you were a truthteller," you reply again.

"And what did I just tell you?" he implores almost inaudibly.

"You said you were a liar," you say.

"Then what must I be?" he whispers.

"You're a liar," you say triumphantly, realizing he has at last told the truth.

And suddenly, magically, the itch has stopped, disappeared, and you release number One who grasps his bruised throat and tries to breathe again. And you see the horrified looks on the faces of number Two and number Three who think you may attack them next. You smile at them and turn and catch the boat back to reality. And that night you sleep peacefully for the first time in thirty years. That sonofabitch liar!

$$\frac{\bullet}{14}$$

$$\frac{\bullet}{\bullet}$$

HOW I
MADE MY
MILLIONS

For some time I have been observing that drivers circling the city streets in search of parking spots behave in a most unfriendly way: "Beat it, Mac, this is my spot!" "Oh, yeah?" "Yeah!" In fact, the mortality rate among spot fighters, as they are called, is probably higher than in any other form of confrontation, husband-and-wife squabbles beginning with "What is this on your collar, dear?" excepted.

Anyway, one day, in a stroke of genius, I decided to hold a

newly opened spot against the cruising throngs and sell it to the highest bidder. Several compacts, J cars, and a Buick had been sniffing around, making passes at me: "Why are you lying in that space, man?" "Hey chief! I'll give you two bucks for that spot." But I held firm, determined to make the best possible sale. Finally, as the bidding became spirited, and tire irons and pipes started to replace the cash being waved in my face, a vintage Rolls offered gold up front and substantial stock to sweeten the deal. Lawyers were summoned, papers signed, and I turned over the spot to the Rolls.

Last summer I hired a team of college kids, at peanut wages, to help locate and hold parking spaces. When we had cornered the market, one of the brighter kids discovered a loophole in the traffic code. Did you know that, while it is not permissible to park in front of a fire hydrant, it is perfectly legal to park over a hydrant? All you need is a hydraulic lift to carry the car above the lift to parking safety. We rent the lifts. A simple maneuver, but one that opened up 12,000 spots in New York City alone.

Today I head Spotco International, which controls 90 percent of the parking spots in this country as well as Europe, Asia, the Middle East, and Africa. Three out of four parking spots that open up anywhere on the globe are picked up by our boys.

Where do I go from here? Sunspots. In this business, you have to think ahead.

NO MORE
"DOING IT"
WITH FROGS

In what has been characterized by liberals as a "barbaric decision," Supreme Court Justice Boris Aurorialis handed down a ruling today which forbids even consenting adults to perform "frogamy," or have intimate relations with frogs. Casual contact was also discouraged. The court held that anyone found plugging a frog or even fondling its bumps could be prosecuted under the new law.

It is no secret that arch-conservative factions on the court view the decision against frogamy as an attempt to stem the tide of the warts epidemic that has been ravishing the country and which they blame on contact with frogs. "Get rid of the little green buggers before they contaminate us all," commented Senator Sten Stennis of South Carolina, one of those who supported the majority decision. "In my home state we keep 'em in swamps and ponds where they belong. We don't bring 'em into the home, ya understand!"

"That's typical bigot talk," said one frogophile all dressed in green. "People like Stennis still don't know the difference between frogs and toads. In his scheme of things, anything that's small and green gives you warts. I'm surprised he's not afraid of olives. The fact is frogs don't give you warts, toads do. Show me one case of warts that was contracted from a frog. Toads, they're the ones," he said.

As was expected, the new law was greeted by a general outpouring of anger and disgust by animal activists, profrog groups, and "frogamours," who hopped around the courthouse in mock-defiance of the landmark ruling before police could capture any of them in nets.

"If you think some black robed justice who probably eats frog's legs at fancy French restaurants is going to tell me how to act with my frog in the privacy of my own bedroom or in my bathtub, you've got another guess coming, bud," said another incensed "froggie."

Nor is the decision likely to curb the growing visibility of home-amphibian contact (frogamy) as a fact of daily life in America, say the experts. The verboten is always desired, and they say, people will probably still go down to the lakes and ponds and swamps in droves to look for that other kind of experience, the kind they can't get at home. Even this evening, after the decision was handed down, one could still observe loose frogs on street corners in major cities, going "gribbet, gribbet" at tourists and passersby, and then leading them off into small hotels and puddles. However, it does weaken the legal arguments of "frogavists" against discrimination.

Sadly the ruling limited past Supreme Court decisions by rejecting what Justice Aurorialis called the view "that any kind of private sexual conduct between consenting adults is constitutionally insulated from state proscription." In his majority opinion Justice Aurorialis asks the difficult question, "What would you do if your son or daughter came home with a dragonfly, for example? And I don't mean to mount in a case."

While the Supreme Court decision was greeted with dismay by froggies, it was certainly the cause for jubilation among a variety of religious and political groups united against homo-frogo love. "I applaud the decision for two reasons," said the Reverend Modus Modandi, head of "The Popular People." "In the first place the highest court has recognized the right of the state to determine its own moral guidelines, that perversion is out of place in our society. And in the second place it sticks it to those froggers. Let them stay with their own species for Christ's sake."

Leaders of interanimal groups and their lawyers said they feared the Supreme Court decision would make it more difficult for them to achieve other objectives, such as custody of tadpoles in mixed marriages, and the rights of frogmen to enter the hop-skip-and-jump event in track meets. They also predicted an upsurge of police harassment against frogomanes as well as dismissals and evictions as a result of the ruling.

Will the Supreme Court decision ultimately change the direction of social and sexual relationships in this country away from homo-frogo love? "I doubt it," said the average man in the street—who, as we talked, just happened to be holding hands and goggling with a real, honest-to-goodness, toad.

$$\frac{\cdot}{16}\frac{}{\cdot}$$

FACT SHEET
ON
<u>ADOLESCENCE</u>

WHAT IS AN ADOLESCENT?

The American adolescent, or "freshmouthicus Americanus," is an ordinary teenager, male or female, who either because of a defective gene or a pernicious virus has somehow gone awry.

ARE THERE ADOLESCENTS IN OTHER COUNTRIES?

Mais oui! They are everywhere. There are British adolescents—"freshmouthicus Brittanicus,"—Japanese adolescents —"freshmouthicus Japanicus," etc.

HOW CAN I TELL AN ADOLESCENT WHEN I SEE HIM?

You can tell the adolescent not so much by the way he or she looks but by the way he slams the door in your face after you have said something which offends him, such as "hello."

IN WHAT WAY HAS HE GONE AWRY?

There are several ways in which he has gone awry. For one thing he eats twelve meals a day instead of three. For another he no longer requires sleep. He can go to bed at 4 A.M. and get up at 7 A.M. and not be any grouchier than usual. Also his intelligence has grown to the point of infinity where he now knows everything, including whatever you were about to say or could possibly think of. But perhaps the most important way in which he has gone awry is the way in which he now talks to you—as if you were no longer his parents but annoying creatures who continue to pest him from the planet, "Stress."

DOES HE RECOGNIZE US AS HIS PARENTS?

No one knows for sure. All that can be said with certainty is that you are a tremendous source of embarrassment to him.

Also, your threats of smacking him and cutting off his allowance if he talks that way to you again will only serve to make him angrier. You are stupid enough as it is.

IN WHAT OTHER WAYS HAS HE CHANGED?

Where once he was polite and well-mannered, he now belches in public. He responds to all questions with terse phrases such as, "Go away!" or "Leave me alone!" He no longer receives homework from school, and when he does, is able to dispatch it in under thirty seconds when you are not looking. He also has scheduled 225 study halls for tomorrow morning just in case, so not to worry. He seeks privacy to the point of reclusion. He has acquired the eating habits of a giant termite. If he continues to grow at the present rate his body will one day be in proportion to his mouth.

WHERE DOES THE ADOLESCENT LIVE?

Male adolescents still tend to live in their rooms, which have alternately been described as lairs or sties. Females may live in their bedrooms, or the bathrooms, or any other part of the house that has a phone and hairdryer, or they may live at their friend's house.

WHAT DOES THE ADOLESCENT DO IN HIS ROOM?

It is believed that he tries to communicate with aliens living in other galaxies by turning up his stereo loud enough so that they can hear it. No one knows for sure if he is successful, but if he isn't, it's because the aliens are deaf.

WHAT DOES THE ADOLESCENT WANT?

The adolescent desperately wants to grow a third ear so that he (she) does not have to remove his Walkman when talking on the telephone.

DO ADOLESCENTS FALL IN LOVE?

Frequently, though not in the same way as you or I.

HOW CAN I TELL IF MY ADOLESCENT IS IN LOVE?

He will display one of the following signs:

1. A tattoo of "Veronica" emblazoned on his chest.
2. Veronica, herself, emblazoned on his chest.
3. A sudden interest in poetry, "Veronica, Veronica, who art thou Veronica?"

WILL BEING IN LOVE AFFECT HIS PERFORMANCE IN SCHOOL?

Only Veronica will affect his performance in school. If you can somehow get to Veronica. Hint: She is very fond of black lipstick.

HOW IS THE ADOLESCENT'S HEALTH DURING THIS PERIOD?

He suffers from a hideous form of body blight (called acne) which he tries to treat by eating enormous amounts of Twinkies and soda.

DOES THIS REMEDY WORK?

It must because he leaves the cans and wrappers all over his room for you to clean up.

IS THERE ANYTHING I CAN SAY OR DO TO GET THROUGH TO THE ADOLESCENT, TO HELP GUIDE HIM THROUGH THIS DIFFICULT PERIOD, TO BE HIS FRIEND?

No!

17

GROWING A LITERARY GARDEN

For some years now, as a city gardener, I have tended a literary garden on my terrace, designed not only for the eye and ear of the present, but for the foreseeable future as well.

In order to achieve this end, I have avoided specialty literature such as verb gardens or beds of just poems, which require a great deal of care and devotion, and tried to provide a balanced garden of mixed genres.

Thus, in the front of my garden along the border I have

placed Elizabethan sonnets in groups of two, with interstices of delicate haiku from Japan. Just behind these attractive blooms are some perennial humor pieces by Benchley, Thurber, and Perelman, as well as a popular new hybrid I developed myself. To the left of the humor, up against the parapet wall and serving as windbreaks for the rest of the garden, are two large and sprawling historical novels with leitmotifs that I have fastened to a trellis so they don't get out of hand. Novels, as you know, must be carefully watched and pruned so as not to grow wild and uncontrollable.

Beneath the novels, arranged in separate tubs, are various short stories, essays, and plays, which I have underplanted with low-keyed satire and nonfiction.

For additional color I have sowed some belles-lettres seeds in the window boxes, which should burgeon quickly and flower by summer.

Literary critics and readers who visit my garden from time to time never fail to ask me if tending a literary garden is truly satisfying and fulfilling. And I invariably reply that not only is it more rewarding than I ever imagined, in a hundred wonderful and different ways, it is my way of life.

18

REHEARSING FOR THE APRIL-IN-PARIS BALL

Today we begin rehearsing for the April-in-Paris Ball. His excellency Pierre d'Abouille and Madame d'Abouille together with his excellency Jacques Louisbelle and Madame Louisbelle, and the Honorable Françoise Le Frankpetit, the minister plenipotentiary and Madame Le Frankpetit will lead the procession of committees in from the antechamber of the grand ballroom of the Waldorf Astoria hotel to the grand ballroom itself which will be decorated in apricot and cream like an enormous soufflé. Space dessert is the theme of this year's ball as you may have guessed and each table will serve as part of an endless array of postprandial confectionary flying saucers. The processional march will be to the accompaniment of the tune, *I Love a Parade,* a particular favorite of his excellency d'Abouille's and Madame d'Abouille's.

The Honorary committee this year, as last, consists of President and Mrs. René Pop of the Cameroons, Ambassador and Mrs. Snipe Villengart, Senator and Mrs. Carter Blinker, the Honorable P. Wimbleton Foote, Mr. and Mrs. Mortimer R. L. Canestilt III, James Goat, Mrs. Hedvig Van Looming, and Mr. and Mrs. Cornelius Ormsby Drillinghaus, though it is rumored that Mrs. Drillinghaus may not make it down from her villa in Los Ojos in time for the ball and will have to be replaced by her understudy, Ms. Coco Le Chien of Park Avenue South, an old friend of Mr. Drillinghaus's.

The junior committee consists of Miss Puff Puff Williger, Ms. Roo Dewing, Pedro de Bova, Ms. Cookie Winsome, Princess Lulu Von Schmidt, Baron Hans Rockport, the Diddle twins, Peter Stick, Ms. Michelle Bird, Ms. Dove Trot, and Count Harry Snortduff.

In any event once in the grand ballroom, Les Comités will goosestep twice around the perimeter of the room never taking their eyes off the person in front of them, then stop, execute a formal half turn to the right, or droit royale, and find their seats at the appropriate disk-shaped table.

It is at this precise moment with the comités seated that the ceiling, powered by two twenty-thousand horsepower motors, will slowly draw open like a giant clam exposing the dark blue heavens to view. Each committee member will fasten his seat belt, recline into take-off position, and proceed through the ceiling in formation toward the stars. Assuming favorable weather conditions, the tables, or ships if you prefer, will rendezvous in earth orbit before beginning their excursion through the solar system climaxing with a midnight dance on the sea floor of Alpha Centauri, and then the return to earth and the Waldorf-Astoria.

At about 4 A.M. les comités will exit the grand ballroom and file into the lobby of the hotel where scrambled eggs, sausages and bacon, pancakes, and other breakfast delicacies will be served. Following breakfast, the revelers will file back into the grand ballroom where, like a cloud of moths, they will consume the soufflé decoration which turns out to be real and good.

At 5:30 A.M. a siren will go off signaling the official end of the ball when each quadrant leader will shepherd his flock to the suites and rooms reserved upstairs in the hotel. Other more ordinary guests will go home to life.

Of course, this is just the rehearsal and the actual festivities will not begin until next Friday night.

My role in the April-in-Paris Ball rehearsal is not exactly a major one. I am a guest of the Orkins, table 243 A in the balcony, and I must practice my "Hi, how're you" smile until I get it just right. Last year, I accidentally gave a "Ho, ho, ho, caught you in the act" smile when I should have given a "Hi, how're you" and was publicly sniffed at. The Orkins suggested I get to practice early this year if I want to remain on their "A" guest list and especially if I want to be seated at a flying table. Since I do, I am practicing as hard as I can. Wish me luck.

19

TARZAN THE APE'S DIARY FOUND

"Cheetah has become indispensable to me. I could use five Cheetahs to peel the fruits, clean the tree house, and serve friends."

The writer, allegedly, is the legendary Tarzan of the Apes. The words, though, are carping and crude, the random droppings of an unlettered man who seems at times to be less a heroic figure than a wimp lost in the jungle.

He frets about his food and digestion and tells on his animal friends leaving trails of petty gossip for us to follow. Yet, what he does write may be of interest to naturalists and un-naturalists alike, for there is also a dark undercurrent of jungle perversion which surfaces in the diary.

Here is Hista, the snake, displaying a sharp intelligence and formidable talent for sizing up edible prey, "Ummmm good, SSSSSSS, Yoiks!" says Hista, throwing up when something she has swallowed is too large for her to digest—in this case Mt. Kilimanjaro.

Yet here is Hista, the snake, in another pose, slithering and alluring at night, "Here TarZZZan, you handsome devil you. Come on over here to Hissssssta. That's it, you know you love it, no need to pretend here in the tree. That's it let me coil around you like I always do, aaaaaah, that's it, faster, faster, faster, . . . aaaaaah, ahhhhh!

Tarzan recalls his first mistress, Oomsluth, with obvious fondness and longing. "She had this glorious hair all over her body from head to tail, and her fangs were the color of burnished gold. She could do things with her tail you can't begin to imagine. Aieeeeee-aaaah!, Aieeeeee-aaaaah!" he volunteers which hitherto Tarzanophiles had understood to be a shriek of triumph.

In any case, to the astonishment of scholars and animals who knew him, it now appears that Tarzan kept a secret handwritten diary from mid–1908 until just shortly before his death last year at the Kampala Home for the Aged where he finished his days sitting on the branch of a tree pretending he was a salt lick.

Through all those years Tarzan scribbled away on tree bark, animal hides, large leaves, and anything else he could find until he had filled something over sixty volumes with that inimitable bush scrawl of his and hidden them under his bed in the toy chest. Most were sealed with tree sap imprinted with a fancy "T" and countersigned by his alter ego,

Cheetah, whom some believe really wrote the diaries. They were flown out of the Belgian Congo (now Zaire) last Fall and housed at the Bronz Zoo in New York until just last week when *Ranger Rick* magazine somehow got a hold of them and released a few excerpts to the public.

"Numa, the lion, is driving me crazy. Slinks around jungle like he owns it. Tarzan own jungle. Tarzan own everything. Tarzan will deal with Numa soon, stick broom handle where Numa no like it."

"Made Jane new loin cloth today with peek-a-boo front for Saturday cookout. Hope Jane like it. Tantor, the Elephant and Horta, the boar cannot make it. Good, Horta smell bad. Beginning to think Tantor is antisocial. Fortunately, that sexy Hista is coming."

Ultimately, the diaries may shed new light on the innermost thoughts and sex life of a man when he is abandoned in the jungle at a tender age and forced to spend his formative years seeking favors from slow birds.

Along with the diaries, *Ranger Rick* has also obtained a vast collection of other volumes containing documents that may prove Tarzan was Jewish and that his last name was not really Greystoke but Zimmerman. Photographs from his bar mitzvah at Temple Emanu-El on Fifth Avenue and a reception later at the Pierre attended by family and friends strongly suggest this.

But are the diaries genuine? Here the scholars divide.

"I would not be surprised to find that the whole thing is a hoax," said Dr. Arnot Rasmussen, professor of physiognomy at the University of Southern California, who has studied men of enormous physiques ad nauseum. "Tarzan would never have bragged about beating up an antelope as he does in volume twenty-six of the diaries," the professor says. "He was a gentleman, not a bully."

"Au contraire," says Dr. René de la Beurre, of the Sorbonne in Paris. "Ze diaries are ze real McCoy as you Americains say. Zey even smell like ze real thing, strong and apey. You can bet wiz me anytime."

Clearly *Ranger Rick* has gone out on a limb with the Tarzan diaries in maintaining their authenticity.

Will the limb break?

Probably only Cheetah knows for sure.

Aieeeeeee-ahhhhhhh!

÷ 20 ÷

WHAT WILL YOU BE IN YOUR NEXT LIFE?

Believe it or not, what you will be in your next incarnation is determined almost entirely by the last two digits of your birth year. Thus, if you happened to be born in 1945, you will be reincarnated as a fly. Yes, a fly. I'm sorry, I know you would rather have come back as a jewel or a Rolls-Royce, but you're quite unmistakably a fly. I've checked my figures a hundred times over. Nineteen forty-five is a fly, a common housefly. Look, it's not as bad as you think—the ability to soar through the air effortlessly, taste a dozen different meals at a single restaurant, buzz. Just watch out for scrolls of sticky paper hanging from the ceilings and swatters and you'll be all right, trust me. And get your nose out of that stuff, right now! Yuck!

In any event, quite obviously not all of you will come back as flies. Many of you will come back as princes, and water lilies, and business moguls with estates on the water in East Hampton and Palm Beach—it's sort of like the lottery, you don't know until your number comes up. But in the interests of the curious, impatient, or just those who have to learn now so they can prepare for the next life, I have set forth the future incarnations of those born in the following years:

1937—'37 was a good year. You will all come back as magnums of Lafite Rothschild wine, the best. Of course you will be different vintages, since you won't all expire at the same time. That's only natural. For what it's worth, 1987, 1992, 2004 will be the great years, and 2007 the very greatest. If you can make it to 2007, by all means do, since you will not only make great drinking at special occasions and society dinners, but set auction records as well. Salud!

1938—Pin Curls. What can I say?

1939—The men of '39 will return as major stakes race-horses who will retire in their prime as studs. The ladies will be brood mares. If you've got any sexual hangups such as fear of doing it in front of other horses, or spectators, get rid of them now. And if I were you, I'd eat lots of fresh figs and oysters. Capice?

1941—Chairs. You will come back as chairs. Arms, Chipendales, Rockers, Queen Annes, Captains. A mixed blessing. Depends on what room you wind up in, and who sits on you. For example, you could be just a bar stool in an Irish pub, God forbid, or the guest chair next to Johnny Carson on the "Tonight Show." As you can see, it's all in the luck of the draw. And in case any of you creative types were wondering, there is a chair in the dressing room of the Dallas Cowgirls upholstered in the finest silk moiré.

1944—You will return as a business tycoon, regardless of whether you are male or female. Deal after deal will turn into success and you will be pictured on the cover of *Time* magazine. So affluent will you become, in fact, that small governments and Adnan Khashoggi will approach you for loans. Women will fall all over you, hypnotized by your power, and strong men will envy you. Unfortunately, you will look like a hemorrhoid. Try to remember the bargain you made with Mephistopheles and improve on it next time.

1949—People born in 1949 will come back as wands. Magic wands, silver wands, bubble wands, glass wands. If you've ever wanted to be a wand, 1949 was the year in which to be born.

1952—Tell the truth, whenever you've thought about reincarnation you've imagined that someone could come back as a butterfly, right? Well, congratulations, those of you born in 1952 actually will. You will be colored like the rainbow, able to ride the wind like a hot-air balloon, and alight as soft as a feather on pollen sweet flowers. Except for you, John. You will be a lunar moth.

1957—Wines of all kinds.

1959—'59s will return as food. Some will be crêpes suzettes, some will be chicken McNuggets, and still others roast beef Hovis sandwiches with the works. It's hard to know in advance just who will be what, but if you have cauliflower ears or are called sugar, honey, or cookie on a regular basis, chances are you have a rough idea where you're heading.

1960—Diamonds—great! What can anyone say if you come back as a diamond? Like the erections of '53, you will be hard.

$$\div$$

21

EXCERPTS FROM *THE FRUMKES BOOK OF RECORDS*

Each year the redoubtable *Guinness Book of Records* sells 18 billion copies in 20 billion languages trumpeting the names of new record holders in every conceivable human condition and competition. Nevertheless, as with any extraordinary undertaking, there occur occasional omissions and ellipses in the Guinness book which only an even more remarkable publication could take account of. I refer, of course, to *The*

Frumkes Book of Records, which, through superhuman effort and scholarship, records for posterity those records somehow missed by the Guinness work. What follows are some of this year's entries from the Frumkes volume.

THE FRUMKES BOOK OF RECORDS

OVERALL RECORDS

HEAVIEST MAN

THE HEAVIEST medically weighed human was the Eskimo Ezuk Kazook who weighed 22,000 pounds. Kazook died in 1926 at the age of twenty-three when he was accidentally harpooned to death while taking a late afternoon swim. The

Scandinavian whaler responsible for the harpooning was so overcome by the error of what he had done that he sold the blubber back to the Eskimos at half price.

FASTEST HUMAN
FOR MANY years it was supposed that Jesse Owens or perhaps a modern-day gold medal Olympic sprinter could be called the world's fastest human. But officially the fastest human turns out to be R. Bernie Allen of East Islip, Long Island, who was clocked by his wife at over 70 mph going from the living room to the bathroom during a severe case of stomach cramps. Mr. Allen was 46 years old at the time.

OLDEST LIVING THING
SOME REPUTABLE scientists claim that the oldest recorded living thing is a bristlecone pine (Pinus Longalva) designated WPN–114, growing at 10,750 feet above sea level on the northeast face of Wheeler Park (13,063 feet) in Eastern Nevada, which according to studies is about 4,900 years old. Others say George Burns.

LONGEST JELLYFISH
THE LONGEST jellyfish ever recorded was *Cyanea arctica*. One specimen washed up on shore in Florida had a bell 7½ feet in diameter and tentacles 120 feet thus giving a theoretical tentacular span of some 245 ft. It was eventually popped by a ten-year-old boy walking along the beach with a stick and yielded twelve quarts of grade A, unrefined raw marmalade.

DENSEST TERRITORY
THE MOST densely populated territory in the world is the Portuguese province of Macau (Or Macao), on the southern coast of China. It has an estimated population of 314,000 (in

1970) in an area of 6.2 square miles, giving a density of about 50,645 per square mile. In graphic terms this is somewhat denser than a subway car and somewhat less dense than a black hole. For the last twenty years Macau has been the first choice of pharmaceutical companies when testing new underarm deodorants.

SPORTS RECORDS

MOST SUCCESSFUL MATADOR
THE MOST successful matador of all time, measured by bulls killed, was Juan "The Butcher" Del Pingo of Madrid, Spain whose lifetime total was seventeen thousand.

Early in his career Del Pingo discovered that bulls were especially susceptible to the .44 magnum which he kept hidden under his cape. Del Pingo met his Waterloo when a bull called "El Braino" (The Smart One) entered the ring wearing a bulletproof vest and chased him into the second tier bleachers. His nerve gone, Del Pingo spent his remaining years fighting chickens at a local poultry farm.

TALLEST BASKETBALL PLAYER
The tallest basketball player ever to have played the game was Harry "Steeple" Bobkin. He stood 11 feet 8 inches at the knee and had to bend down in a crouch to dunk baskets. In his twilight years, Bobkin was hired by the Civil Aeronautics Commission as a pylon.

MOST AVERAGE BATTER
The most average batter of all time was Ron "Eh!" Harrisplugger who batted average in over 300 games with the St. Louis Leaflets. So middle-of-the-road was Harrisplugger's batting, record books have him batting average 50 percent of

the time. When he wasn't batting average Harrisplugger could be found sitting on a fence.

FASTEST SWIMMER

The fastest swimmer on record is, surprisingly, not Johnny Weissmuller or Mark Spitz, but Hugo Von Bunt of East Germany, who earlier this year outdistanced an Italian-made speedboat in a five-lap race across the Mediterranean. Scientists are trying to determine whether Von Bunt's insatiable craving for diesel fuel and methyl alcohol has anything to do with his speed.

COMMUNICATIONS RECORDS

THE LONGEST TELEPHONE CALL

The longest telephone call of all time was between Pete "The Mouth" Lambruzzi of Wamsutta, Michigan, and his girl, Honey Sue Melon of Peoria, Illinois. So long was the call that while it began on the evening of June 2nd, 1977, it has yet to end. What annoys Pete's parents the most about the call, aside from the bill, is that they have been waiting five years now to call the McDermotts and tell them dinner is off.

BEST SELLING BOOK

Despite the fact that most people have heard *The Bible* is the world's best selling book, or in some quarters *How to Cure a Rash with Vitamin E*, the actual best-selling book of all time is *Linda's Strange Vacation*, the underground classic by Marcus Van Dang. It has been estimated that between 1800 and 1975 some two billion copies were printed and circulated, mostly in the South Bronx, and that certain sections have received more close scrutiny than lines 1–8 of the U.S. tax form.

The most famous passage in the book is that which begins: "And Linda walked through the gate into what at first appeared to be a giant asparagus patch...."

MOST SENSITIVE RECEIVER

The most sensitive receiving instrument in the world is not, as you might suspect, the dish radio telescope in Areceibo, Puerto Rico, nor the Early Bird radar warning system ringing Iceland, nor even the delicate sonar device found in most modern submarines. Rather it is the human ear—or more specifically, the human ear of Mrs. Maudy Polesnipper, the Brandywine, Missouri, town gossip who can pick up even a whispered rumor at 2–200 miles, urban areas included. Got that Maudy?

INSURANCE RECORDS

MOST FREQUENT SETTLEMENT

Lloyd's of London, known throughout the world as an insurer of last resort, has just recently insured a Mr. Pearson Dummel of East Wyltwick, New Zealand, against insults directed against him by his wife, Gorgon. To date, Lloyd's has daily had to settle insult claims with Dummel, thereby making his coverage the most frequently settled of all time. For the record, Mr. Dummel's annual premiums for this insurance do not exceed this country's gross national product by more than two or three billion dollars, if that much.

THE SMALLEST LIFE POLICY

The smallest life insurance policy ever sold to an individual was one for two cents, sold to Eddy Fluecklin of Brooklyn, New York, who had recently welched on a debt owed to friends in the underworld named "Steel Tony" and "Max the

Plumber." The figure, two cents, was objectively arrived at by a panel of Bulgarian actuaries asked to evaluate Fluecklin's chances of surviving the week. The life insurance company issuing the policy, agreed.

LARGEST POLICY
The largest insurance policy on record is that taken out by the United States government on the country insuring us against devastation by nuclear attack. In the event of internecine war it is comforting to know that we are all insured by Swiss insurance companies and that if we survive, we will also probably collect. Now don't you feel better?

MOST SALES
The agent who sold more insurance than anyone on record is Kenny Teagueform of Butte, Montana, who for a period of ten years, 1957–67, sold more than $100,000,000 worth of life insurance to the local residents each year. Kenny credits his good fortune to his personality and the technique he developed of shoving a loaded .45 double magnum inside the mouth of a prospective insuree while soliciting him. Although he is very rich, Kenny is serving consecutive fifty-year terms in the Montana State penitentiary for having finished off two individuals who resisted his sales pitch.

WOMEN'S RECORDS

MOST PROVOCATIVE QUESTION ASKED BY WIVES OF THEIR HUSBANDS
While there are many provocative questions which can be posed in the various theatres of human discourse, the most provocative on all counts is that posed by the average wife to

her husband: "Do you think Gladys, (substitute Conchita, Susan, Helga, Maxine, etc.) is attractive?"

This virulent question, according to experts, has been responsible, as of July 1982, for 36,000,000 cases of divorce, 67,000 homicides, and 96,000,000 purchases of 14–karat gold earrings.

MOST BEAUTIFUL WOMAN

The question, "Who is the most beautiful woman in the world?" is a trick question since beauty is almost entirely subjective. Mark Antony thought Cleopatra was the most beautiful woman in the world; Akhenaten, Nefretete. Actually, the most beautiful woman in the world today is Pachysandra Dufsnort of Minneapolis, Minnesota—but her name is so off-putting.

RICHEST WOMAN

The richest woman in the world is, without question, Mrs. Barbara Annis Rockefeller Mellon Hunt Getty de Medici, whose fortune has been conservatively estimated at 10^{63} or 1,000,000,000,000,000,000,000,000,000, etc., dollars. Mrs. de Medici is so rich that for six months now she has had practically no difficulty in meeting the maintenance charges on her studio apartment in Manhattan. That's what I call rich!

MOST CHILDREN

The record for the most children belongs to Mrs. Clarence C. Hinxstermullin of Memphis, Tennessee, who, at last count, had 426 children ages one through fifteen. In all fairness to other persons who may be trying for the record, it must be said that Mrs. Hinxstermullin considers pencils to be children too, and that 423 of her children are stamped #2 just under their erasers.

TRAVEL RECORDS

THE MOST EXCITING CITY
The most exciting city in the world is undoubtedly White Plains, New York, where on any given day, summer or winter, one can find several stores open as well as a few restaurants and movie theatres. The second most exciting city is reputed to be Paris after dark.

LONGEST CRUISE
The longest cruise ever recorded was the one taken by Captain Nemo on the *Nautilus* for fifty-six years. Unfortunately, Nemo's Dramamine ran out after year one, and he spent the next fifty-five years hanging over the starboard rail. The magnitude of Nemo's achievement becomes apparent when one considers the *Nautilus* was a submarine.

MOST MILES LOGGED
The most miles ever logged by an amateur world traveler was two billion, four hundred thirty million, eight hundred sixty-seven thousand, two hundred twelve, by Stanislaus Shoesniffer of Peoria, Illinois, who accidentally caught his tie in a Saturn II rocket bound for the planet Neptune. When last heard from, somewhere between Orion, the Hunter and The Great Crab Nebula, Shoesniffer was on the verge of working his tie free.

TALLEST HOTEL IN THE WORLD
The tallest hotel in the world is the Sears Tower in Chicago, 110 stories high, standing, 1,454 feet. Sadly, most people who occupy the Sears tower don't even realize it's a hotel. The second tallest hotel is the World Trade Center in New

York City. For what it's worth, the smartest hotel in the world is the Ritz in Paris, which has an I.Q. of 146.

HEALTH RECORDS

OLDEST PERSON
The greatest authenticated age to which a human has ever lived is 310 years. Pierre Rangoon, a French Canadian health buff, was active up until the day he died spending the last hundred years of his life as an "objet d'art" in his great-grand-daughter's apartment. He attributed his great longevity to hard work, abstinence from cigarettes and alcohol, and having lost his birth certificate at the age of 25.

WORST INSOMNIAC
The worst insomniac of all time is thought to be Count Dracula of Transylvania, who never slept a night of his life. For years he reputedly stayed up through the wee hours watching late show after late show and hundreds of sermonettes until he was so sick of them he could throw up. Only the commercial breaks, during which he would run out of the house to suck the blood of friends and neighbors, provided him with any relief. The Count finally found lasting peace when an uncooperative guest, who was to be a late-night snack, drove a stake through his heart.

WORST ALLERGIC REACTION
The worst allergic reaction was suffered by David "The Parrot" Lane of Louisville, Kentucky, during the hayfever season of 1971, when his nose, usually two inches long swelled to 4½ feet, root to tip. While the nose was thus swollen, Mr. Lane sneezed violently, blowing the roof off a neighbor's house and exceeding six on the Richter scale. His nose never

did return to its normal size and he is often mistaken for a tripod.

LARGEST APPENDIX
The largest appendix ever removed was a six foot, 210 pound behemoth from a woman four feet tall weighing 102 pounds. In an unusual landmark decision, the surgeon-in-chief at the hospital where the appendectomy was performed decided that he had really removed the woman from the appendix and threw the woman away.

BEST PHYSIC
The best physic ever concocted was a mixture of bad tunafish salad and prune juice devised by scientists at the Bell Telephone labs in Matawan, New Jersey. When tested on a clogged elephant at the Bronx Zoo, the results were almost biblical.

"A low rumbling could be heard in the East like the angry beating of a thousand wings. This was accompanied by sudden flashes of lightning which lit up the sky like the dawning of a new day, and then . . . . for forty days and forty nights."

The physic is expected to be marketed next year for humans under the label "Vavoom!" by Hoffman La Roche.

ANOTHER NEW TAX PLAN

WASHINGTON

In a bold and controversial move President Bush has appointed the Sheriff of Nottingham as his new Secretary of the Treasury, and the Sheriff in turn has unveiled a new tax plan to replace the one that has just become law. Under the plan, current rates of taxation for high, middle, and low income residents would fall to practically nothing from the present rates. For example, a family living in any major urban city with an annual income of $25,000 and typical deductions would keep all $25,000, according to the Sheriff's proposal. A family earning $100,000 would keep all $100,000. However, in the new proposal, the President would reserve the right to accuse certain individual taxpayers of treason and/or lawbreaking and seize his home and all his goods. In addition, the lawbreaking individual would be branded an "outlaw" and anyone who killed him would be rewarded, the plan states.

"How then would the administration succeed in raising sufficient funds to offset the growing national debt?" asked one reporter.

"Silence, you dog!" replied the Sheriff of Nottingham, striking the reporter roughly across his insolent mouth.

"Once the President seized a man's lands," explained the Sheriff after cooling down, "he would put one of his consituents in the man's place—provided the constituent paid the administration large sums of money. It would not matter how the constituent came by this money. In fact the easiest way would be to take it from small businessmen, farmers, and shopkeepers. In addition," he continued, "developers, bankers, and other high-level industrial types in league with the administration would also have the right to take property when they so desired. In this way enormous revenues would accrue to the government, more even than under the present tax system."

A special enforcer commission, consisting of police, CIA operatives, and mafia strong arms, would be established to oversee the collection of monies and keep order.

Generally speaking, the higher the individual's status and income, the less likely it was that he would be declared an outlaw and his property confiscated, an analysis showed. Persons at this level are usually sheltered by influence and powerful lawyers. Conversely, families earning between $12,000 and $24,000 per annum would be more vulnerable to having their properties seized under the new plan. Thus, there would be an increased incentive for lower income families to move up to a higher bracket.

Critics of the Sheriff's tax proposals say the new plan would be cruel and unjust, that the very notion of forcing money from individuals weaker than oneself, no matter how tempting, runs contrary to conventional democratic philosophy. They say that under the Sheriff's plan all that will happen is that seeds of discontent will be sewn among the people and that certain brave individuals will band together in the woods and fight the Sheriff and President Bush tooth and nail. They point out that representative Locksley of Sherwood Forest has already introduced a counterproposal in the house which advocates appropriating from the rich and giving to the poor, those on welfare, and those with incomes below $5,000 per year.

COMPARING THE PROPOSED TAX LAWS (INDIVIDUAL RATES)

OLD TAX LAW
15 brackets
from 11% to
50% (Single)

CURRENT TAX LAW
0% up to $2,800 of (AGI)
15% up to $19,000
25% up to $38,100
35% over $38,000

SHERIFF OF NOTTINGHAM
0% from lowest to highest
brackets unless you are
considered an outlaw in which
case rates are 100% plus
all your goods and your
home—maybe your life.

LOCKSLEY
0% if you are poor or on welfare.
100% if your income is over $50,000
or if you smell of money.

Locksley has gone on record as saying that if necessary he
will lead his merry constituents in the woods against the administration.

Observers here and abroad see a major battle shaping up
between the followers of Locksley and the President over the
Sheriff's new tax plan.

As if to start things rolling, the Sheriff, this day, declared
Locksley an outlaw—and was rewarded with an arrow
through his hat.

$$\overset{\bullet}{\underset{\bullet}{23}}$$

BORING NOVELS FOUND TO CONTAIN TRYPTOPHANE

Why do some books put us to sleep and others not? This question has been plaguing publishers, marketing experts, and sleep researchers for decades.

It has long been known, for example, that big historical novels read just before bedtime quickly lull the reader into a deep, untroubled, stage-4 sleep. Yet just why this happens, no one knows. Is it that these novels are heavy, sometimes weighing ten or fifteen pounds or more, and sooner or later all on the reader's head knocking him unconscious? Or is it that large novels are often boring and tedious, hypnotizing the reader into a presleep trance by endlessly introducing new characters and plot variations, until his mind simply closes down?

For years scientists believed that these reasons explained the "dull novel, doze off" phenomenon, but they were not totally convinced. Now new evidence suggests that boring novels may contain tryptophane, an essential amino acid occurring in the seeds of some leguminous plants, and released from proteins by tryptic digestion. Tryptophane is an amazing substance. Laboratory experiments have shown that rats eating tryptophane tend to live three times as long as those eating only cyanide. Tryptophane is a natural sedative, a soporific that puts you to sleep. Ho, hummmm! I'm yawning now just thinking about it, though it could be my prose. These scientists believe that people trying too hard to devour a boring book or digest the material in it may release the tryptophane sending them into a glazy stupor. Tryptophane is also found in turkey which explains why so many people leave the Thanksgiving dinner table stuffed and promptly fall asleep on the living room couch.

"C'mon Jim, wake up, it's time to leave. Wake up, everybody left two hours ago."

But the question still remains, why do certain books and even sentences from those books apparently contain tryptophane, while others do not?

"In fact, the parliament of 1265, which lasted into March, accomplished a great deal," is full of tryptophane, while...

"She was merely an object of pleasure, a sexual distraction, a sorceress," has none.

You can almost tell right off which sentences are loaded with tryptophane and which ones aren't. Why don't you try.

> a. "My friends, if I am elected..."
> b. "You are talking about Chantepie, I am certain," said M. Verdurin, as he came toward us.
> c. "The one opened the door with a latchkey and went in, followed by a young fellow who awkwardly removed his cap."

What do you mean, you're not sure? The "a" sentence has tryptophane written all over it, you dodo. The other two are Proust and Jack London. My God!

At the twenty-fifth floor biological booklab of Simon & Schuster publishers in New York, Dr. Laura Yorke, director of research, speculates that perhaps the boring books are really "turkeys" in the figurative sense, which would account for the release of the relaxing amino acid. Spokespersons at Barnes and Noble are not so sure,

"Books with dates and history just bore the hell out of people," says Harold Barnes & Noble, son of the founder. "They can't assimilate all the material, so they go to sleep."

Nevertheless, researchers have deduced that historical tomes, short story collections, self-indulgent, autobiographical novels, especially ones entitled *Me*, and scientific books about Blodgett's disease, contain large amounts of tryptophane which often puts even the author himself to sleep zzzzzzzzzzzzz. This information has helped the publishers who now encourage their authors to have their novels tested for tryptophane before they submit them.

Conversely, the researchers have found that the majority of people stay awake reading novels which contain lots of sex, violence, and romance. Thus, they have concluded that steamy sex, violence, and dreamy goo-goo novels, must contain very little tryptophane if any at all. Dr. Yorke adds that S&S now routinely screens their books for traces of tryptophane, and if any is found they expunge those books immediately from their lists. This may help explain why all you see in bookstores these days are ménage à trois love manuals, Barbara Cartland novels, and stick-um, stab-um thrillers.

Can scientists extrapolate from books to other areas? Will boring movies, plays, and operas ultimately be found to contain tryptophane? Will you be found to have high levels of tryptophane in your blood, as I suspect? These are provocative questions that only time will answer.

$$\dot{\overline{24}}_\bullet$$

HALLOWEEN
HOROSCOPE

Near the end of the month, as the full harvest moon sprays the air full of bats and the leaves disappear from the trees, eerie things begin to happen. Pumpkins rise up from the fields and find their way to your home at night along with ghosts, goblins, banshees, and assorted rattletrap skeletons and black cats. Do not panic. Help will come in the form of little orange, yellow, and white pellets called "chicken corn."

Gather these up wherever you can find them—usually in

candy stores and supermarkets—and cleverly place them in plastic bowls in front of your home. They will save you from unspeakable pranks and insults on the night of the 31st. A jack-o'-lantern in your window will also help. These things, alas, do not work to ward off I.R.S. agents, who simply laugh sadistically whenever they see chicken corn. Fortunately, you have until April to prepare for *them*.

Should you survive All Hallow's Eve with but minor damage to your home and soul, you can probably look forward to a relatively tranquil November. I see only turkeys and Squanto in the weeks ahead. Use this time to find out who Squanto was.

25

HOLIDAY SUCCESS AND THE ART OF EXECUTIVE GIFTMANSHIP

Well, the holiday season is upon us and the spirit of Xmas, like Puck in *Midsummer Night's Dream,* moves easily through the boardrooms and executive chambers of corporate New York casting spells and causing otherwise prudent men to take leave of their senses and make gifts to one another of incredible largesse.

"Harry, old pal, because we've been partners for twenty-two years I am making you a gift of 220,000 shares of Beamish Corporation through our new stock option plan. The one our brilliant accountant, Crosby, has just put in place."

"Barry, old buddy, that's terrific. And because I feel special affection for you, too, after all these years together, I am making you a gift of 220,000 shares of Beamish Corporation as well. Let's say we toast the holiday season and Crosby. To Crosby..."

I have in mind also the little trinkets these CEOs give to encourage their employees to work harder, or as an appreciation. Take, for example, the diamond necklace J. Wallace Pratherwood III gave to Ms. Lulu LaBelle, his secretary of two weeks to help increase her typing speed, or the 54 foot yellow sail boat, "Lulu's Dream," he gave her as a reward for using carbons in all her correspondence. Ms. LaBelle was so overwhelmed by these generous gifts that she promptly sued Mr. Pratherwood for paternity.

However not all corporate gift giving is self serving or fraught with danger. Most gifts, in fact, are given to executives and are purely motivated and intended to express the giver's respect and admiration for the givee. Gifts also help chase the blues at this time of year and are more welcome in most offices than Valia (plural of Valium—only dummies say Valiums) or booze.

"God, I'm depressed."

"Cheer up Mr. Thornton. Look what just came in the mail —a new set of quoits from Dexter Woolmitten."

"Thank heaven. I feel better already."

Thus there are certain guidelines that I have laid down to help you select the right corporate gift during this holiday season. Follow these guidelines carefully and you will be rewarded with the acknowledgment and gratitude that are your due.

BE ORIGINAL

On first glance it might seem appropriate to give Lee Iacocca an automobile for a holiday gift. After all, Mr. Iacocca works in the automotive industry, understands the inner workings of a car, and presumably drives. But will he remember your gift when everyone and his uncle is giving him a car? Was it the Ford Mustang, the Mercedes, or the BMW that you gave him? He won't remember. And who can blame him. You must be original with your presentation to Lee Iacocca so that your gift will stand out among the many. Men like Iacocca are sick of cars. A garage, however, he will remember. Give Lee Iacocca a garage.

The same applies to Donald Trump. He's got co-ops coming out of his nose. He probably receives more co-ops as gifts than he builds. Give him something original. Give him Lee Iacocca.

BE SURE YOUR GIFT IS IN GOOD TASTE

No matter how much you spend on your gift and no matter how lovely it is, it will be looked on with disfavor if it is not in good taste. Thus, it is considered inappropriate to present the CEO of a major corporation with a ten-foot nude marble statue of yourself, even if it is carved by Praxiteles. He may think you are fawning, or coming on, or, sorry to have to say it—certifiable. He will be right. What are you? A nut, or something?

PURCHASE YOUR GIFT AT AN EXCLUSIVE STORE

Where you purchase your gift makes all the difference. A gift that is delivered in a robin's egg blue box from Tiffany's or a silver package from Bergdorf Goodman bespeaks class. Let's be honest, it says you spent at least fifty bucks.

"Okay, folks, let's open our gifts. Here Miriam, here's one for you in a blue Tiffany box. Wow, Miriam, someone out there cares. Tiffany's, whooo, whooo, whooo! Oh Miriam, how beautiful! Let's see who it's from.

"Your turn now Jack. What's this? A bag from McDonald's with a large brownish stain. Omigod it's leaking. Get it away from me, Jack, quick. Yuck!"

Poor Jack. When everybody's getting gifts from Saks Fifth Avenue, Dunhill, Mark Cross, and Gucci, a cheeseburger from McDonald's just doesn't make it, even if it is a quarter pounder.

IF IT IS FOR A FEMALE EXECUTIVE ENCLOSE A PERSONAL NOTE WITH THE GIFT

Never send a card that says, "Guess Who?" It is impersonal and invariably the person receiving the gift will not guess that it is from you. She will guess that it is from Artie Waxdriver, your rival, and the guy you can't stand. Come right out and tell her you sent the gift, but in a low-keyed dignified way.

"Cherie! It is from me, your little Pishkin, Davsypoop."

Nauseating as this is, it never fails to win points.

IF IT IS A MALE EXECUTIVE ALSO ENCLOSE A PERSONAL NOTE

If you don't, Artie Waxdriver will definitely take credit. Waxdriver is ambitious and ruthless. He hates you. He wants your job. Go him one better!

"Dear Mr. Marvin,
Merry Xmas. Whatever Waxdriver gave you, double it.

Your faithful servant,

Terry"

MAKE SURE THE GIFT FITS THE EXECUTIVE

While the right gift to an executive will cause him to look with favor upon you and secure your position in the company, the wrong gift will surely undo you. Accordingly, it is a bad decision to give a pink tutu to a vice-president who was formerly the nose tackle for the Chicago Bears. On the other hand it is a good decision to give him a tackling dummy, especially one painted to look like a Redskins tight end or another vice-president.

WHAT TO GIVE, AND WHAT NOT TO GIVE YOUR FAVORITE EXECUTIVE

By now you should be aware that the executive is a special breed of individual. He has achieved success in business through hard work and acumen. He expects a holiday gift that reflects this status. Anything less is to insult him. A new saddle for his polo pony makes a fine gift, as does a custom shotgun made in England or a hand-carved chess set. A league bowling ball, on the other hand is out, too blue collar, as is a rectal thermometer, even if it is gold-plated. The following is a list of gifts that are okay to give an executive, and some to stay away from:

OKAY TO GIVE: Crystal balls; town houses; car phones; leather-bound first editions; Nautilus machines; mistresses;

power boats; power anything; personalized golf club covers; travel valets; lifetime subscriptions to Crain's *New York Business;* shares of stock; fine wines; cameras; electronic gadgets; desk sets; tax advice.

DO NOT GIVE: Parrot suits; nose studs; tattoos; Rambo dolls; bungee cords; mail-order sushi; wax lips; pogo sticks; good seats for jury duty; rubber bathtub or bedroom toys; pet frogs; combat boots; litigation repellent; scholarships to Weight Watchers; earrings (especially for only one ear); Mohammed Ali Rope-a-Dope sets; "Macho Musk" cologne.

A FINAL WORD OF ADVICE

Remember, an executive never opens his own gift. His secretary opens it for him. Therefore, if you are sending a gift to an executive, include a little something for his secretary too. A crisp new twenty dollar bill or bottle of perfume will suffice. As Walt Whitman once observed, "The fastest way to an executive's heart, is through his secretary" (*Leaves Of Grass,* page 86).

And may "Harold," the god of good credit be with you this holiday season.

26

THE FRUMKES CIRCLE

Lewis and Alana Frumkes have let it be known that there is an opening in their immediate circle of friends for another couple, something which occurs no more than once every five or ten years. This unique opportunity and outrageous development can come about only when one of the charter couples decides to drop from the circle. In this case, let us say there has been a *de facto* resignation by the Harvey Bellsmiths.

HISTORY

Apparently, the Bellsmiths had invited the Frumkeses to their country home on a specific weekend as houseguests and forgotten that they had done so. They then invited the Clifton Haggerdorns instead, and when the Frumkeses called about arrangements, Nilly Bellsmith just pretended that the Frumkes invitation had only been tentative.

Suffice it to say that Alana Frumkes received this news with incense, and Nilly Bellsmith got huffy and defensive. And while attempts were made at reconciliation, the strain is now palpable and the friendship is effectively over. Neither couple will come out and say so, of course, but neither will they call each other or invite the other anywhere. And now the Frumkeses have decided to fill the Bellsmith space in their circle of friends.

THE FRUMKES CIRCLE OF FRIENDS

Included in the Frumkes circle of friends, which, incidentally, is considered one of the best and which took the Frumkeses years to cultivate, are the Godsticks, he's the orthopaedic surgeon and polo player, she's the socialite and reading teacher; the Drizzlesnorts, he's the art dealer to the four hundred who at any given time can recall 200–300 ethnic jokes, she's a world-class shopper; Betsy Prixx and Giovanni Rojo, she's the PR brains behind anyone you've ever heard of, he's the photographer and *bon vivant;* Dick Gilbert and Zena, he struck it rich in jeans, she's gorgeous; Siobhan Swandelake, another great beauty and eligible; and Peter Green of Quinta Verde Stables. Then there are the Von Toons, he's the Wall Street mogul, she hypnotizes men like Medusa; six top-flight psychiatrists (two Freudian analysts, two behaviorists, two eclectics) and their wives; and a theoretical physicist. Representing the arts are a dozen assorted writers and poets of secure reputation; two sculptors and a painter; three filmmakers; and a prima ballerina with the New York City Ballet; and two critics. From politics and government: two state senators and a half dozen councilmen. From the halls of power (national and international) two—four secret lobbyists.

WHY YOU WOULD WANT TO JOIN

Apart from the very real claim you could make that you are on a first-name basis with Alana and Lewis Frumkes or any of the other members of their circle of friends, there are tangible benefits to be derived from having joined the Frumkes circle.

It is said that within three calls made by the friends you could reach anyone in the country, including the President himself, the Secretary of State, or the Maître d' at Le Cirque.

The friends' homes are your homes; their friends your friends. When in Southampton, for example, you could call the Gilberts and be invited to lunch at their Joseph Pricci-decorated summer estate on Mecox Bay, the one that has the whole community goggling and waiting for invitations. Or you could call them in Palm Beach, Vail, Saratoga, or Manhattan, or you could call the Drizzlesnorts in Greenwich, or Alan Williams, or Robin Rue, or Jonathan Sale in London, etc.

Nor is there a reason any longer to be a pariah. Your evenings will be filled with dinner parties, barbecues, and wife swaps—your days spent lolling around the pools of the various friends' clubs.

Need I say more? When you are a member of the Frumkes

circle of friends their friends are your friends, you can and should use them to the fullest. That is the way of the circle. Your star is sure to rise.

HOW TO JOIN

Joining the Frumkes circle is not easy, as you would expect. The circle is exclusive and desirable after all. But you understand that. You must be upbeat, personable, loyal, amusing or intelligent (not both), and have contributed something significant to society. You must be honest (at least with the friends), not prone to breaking dates, unenvious, certainly unobvious, and willing to do anything when called upon to help one of the friends. Failure to do so will be dealt with harshly. The Pixleys refused a favor to a friend last year and were drummed out of the circle before they could say, "But..." In such situations there is no quarter shown. Still, you have to have these qualities and adhere to these rules to join any of the better circles these days.

What makes the Frumkes circle special and different from the other circles is that you do have a chance. If you pass muster with the admissions committee, the Van Toons and the Drizzlesnorts, you are in, regardless—and their decision is based entirely on whim.

So be smart, apply now before the Bellsmiths and the Frumkeses make up.

Director of Admissions
The Frumkes Circle
Box 2476, Bell Street Station
New York, N.Y. 11007

$$\frac{\cdot}{27}$$
$$\frac{\cdot}{\text{\tiny ♦}}$$

THE
ALL-AMERICAN
DIET

Thank God, America is still light year's ahead of the rest of the world in diet technology. Every day thousands of hopeful fatties from other countries whose immunity to bread, potatoes, and whipped cream has broken down, hurl themselves on to railroad cars, boats, and airplanes and make their way to our shores, confident that American know-how will help them shed pounds.

But people are notoriously different from one another, and what works for one will not necessarily work for the next. Some people are hooked on grits, while others love fish and chips. Thus, it was only natural that I should develop the All-American Diet to take account of the needs of blubber-balls from all over the country, from Los Angeles to Salt Lake City to the Great White Way. If you can't find a diet that suits you here, you're in a lot of trouble buddy!

So dig in, digest what you read, then choose the diet that's just right for you. *No one doesn't lose on the All-American Diet.*

THE SOUTH BRONX DIET

The South Bronx diet is a radical approach to dieting in which you literally burn the calories right off your body. According to the pyros who developed the diet, you simply douse yourself with kerosene and light a match. Fat will disappear in a flash.*

* There is no maintenance with the South Bronx diet.

THE LAS VEGAS DIET

For an almost sure-fire, quick loss diet, nothing beats the Las Vegas diet. Instead of chips you bet your meals at the crap table and eat your heart out instead of food. If you hit accidentally you get doubles but only two out of a hundred people ever do. One poor soul I watched last week was down to his last piece of sugarless gum when he crapped out. He may have been forlorned but he looked terrific.

MONDAY

Breakfast: Bet bacon and eggs on the 5 & 7. Orange juice on the field.
Lunch: Roast beef sandwich on the pass line.
Dinner: Steak and potatoes on the come line.

TUESDAY

Breakfast: Bacon and eggs on the 5 & 7. Juice on the field.
Lunch: Tuna salad on Big 8.
Dinner: Veal Paprikas on 12 the hard way, 7 & 5.

WEDNESDAY

Breakfast: Bacon and eggs on 5 & 7. Juice on the field.
Lunch: Franks and beans on "Don't Pass."
Dinner: Chicken and rice on snake eyes.

THURSDAY (BINGE DAY)

Press all bets.

THE LOS ALAMOS DIET

For explosive weight loss try the Los Alamos diet, a favorite of physicists for decades. First, line the stomach with liquid hydrogen, tritium, and deuterium so as not to injure delicate abdominal tissue, then swallow a subcritical mass of uranium 235. When ready, swallow the other subcritical mass and brace yourself. As the mushroom cloud clears, pounds will vaporize into thin air.

THE MIAMI BEACH DIET

Formerly known as the "Prune" diet, the Miami Beach diet is a low calorie, high laxative diet which depends for its success on a healthy intestinal tract. Do not stay on the Miami Beach diet for more than two weeks as there is a major chance of turning inside out.

Monday:	Breakfast—one prune
	Lunch—nothing
	Dinner—nothing
Tuesday:	Breakfast—one prune
	Lunch—nothing
	Dinner—nothing
Wednesday:	Breakfast—nothing
	Lunch—one prune
	Dinner—nothing
Thursday:	Binge day, all the prunes you can eat.
Friday:	Breakfast—nothing
	Lunch—nothing
	Dinner—one prune
Weekend:	Tie off your colon until Monday.

THE WASHINGTON, D.C. DIET

The Washington, D.C. diet maintains that if you really comprehend what's going on in the world today, you not only won't want to eat, you will probably want to give back what you have already eaten. To this end, it is important on the Washington, D.C. diet to buy a newspaper and digest as many stories as you possibly can until you begin to feel nauseated. When this point arrives you should fold the paper into a cone and proceed to lose weight.

MONDAY

Breakfast: Assorted troubles around the globe. Black coffee or tea.
Lunch: A bank failing.
Dinner: A space mishap; two muggings or a rape.

TUESDAY

Breakfast: Assorted troubles around the globe. Black coffee or tea.
Lunch: A minor war; news about AIDS.
Dinner: Stock market closings; an air crash.

WEDNESDAY

Breakfast: Assorted troubles around the globe. Black coffee or tea.
Lunch: The economic outlook; two small craft warnings.
Dinner: President's State of the Union message; an explosion.

THURSDAY

Cone day.

FRIDAY

More cone day.

THE FIFTH AVENUE DIET

The beauty of the Fifth Avenue diet is its utter simplicity.

You may eat as much as you want of the following foods—but only these foods:

1. Fresh Iranian beluga caviar
2. Château Lafite-Rothschild 1961
3. Prime ribs of beef
4. Châteaubriand
5. Pâté de foie gras (Strasbourg)
6. Tiptree, little scarlet jam

Since normal mortals cannot afford to subsist on these foods, they will go hungry for the duration of the diet and burn calories like crazy.

28

FRUMKES'S XMAS GUIDE TO TOYS

But first some random thoughts about children and toys: children are attracted to toys much in the way that people starving on the rice diet at Duke University are attracted to roast beef sandwiches with the works; they don't exactly need them, but if you look the other way they will slit your throat from ear to ear in exchange for one. "Sorry, Dad, it was you or the giant Legos."

Without toys children are in danger of becoming, dare I say it, "bored," a fate clearly worse than death.

"I wanna toy, I'm bored!"
"Why not read a book, Figaro, dear."
"A book? Yuck! Books are boring, they remind me of school."
"How about your computer, Darling? Why don't you work on your computer?"
"I don't want to work on my computer. It bores me."
"What about..."
"No, no, no. I'm bored. Bored to tears."

At this point, bored to tears, the child begins to metamorphose right before your eyes. It is an amazing transformation. What was once a sweet freckle-faced little child often mistaken for a dumpling, now begins to grow ears that are perceptibly longer and pointed. Coarse hair starts to sprout on his face and body. Fangs erupt from his mouth. His eyes grow small, red, and beady. They dart around the room searching for toys. He becomes a feral, primitive beast, pawing the ground and snorting with rage. Foam flecks his lips. Unless you carry tranquilizer darts on your person or an FAO Schwarz charge card, you are in serious trouble.

In fact recent thinking has it that Dr. Jekyll was never really suffering from lycanthropy, he was just bored to tears.

Be that as it may, I have also noticed that children prefer very different types of toys, at least that is the case with my brood. Girls tend to like small, soft, or cuddly toys, or jewelry, while boys are into sports stuff and heavy metal.

My daughter, for example, has always been attracted to miniatures, cute wee little things made for Lilliputians or dwarfs. She has tiny little rabbits and tiny little cats, tiny little furniture and tiny little books. When you enter her room you think you may have drunk too much of that new light Moselle the night before. Her room is festooned with stuffed animals; monkeys and bunnies, and chickens and pandas. Maybe she is planning to become a taxidermist.

The only thing stuffed in my son's quarters is my son who has just finished twelve cans of soda and a package of Twinkies. I say "just" because it really doesn't matter when you go in, he will just have finished twelve cans of soda and a package of Twinkies. His choice of toys, however, is definitely different from my daughter's. He is into war weapons and poison gas, hideous devices that can obliterate planets, and enemies, and ultimately his room. Teams from urban renewal arrive weekly to try and reconstruct his room from the debris. If the toys don't do it, the two million decibels emanating from his stereo will. The Voice of America has been studying his speakers for two years trying to figure out where he gets his power. And yes, like all boys my son likes footballs and bats. He displays them attractively on top of his lamp, on the floor as you walk in the door, and in his bathroom sink—right next to the green gooey gunk.

But whatever happened to the friendly toys of yesteryear? BB guns and beanbags and Raggedy Ann dolls; those ubiquitous pink rubber balls that you found in the basement and played stickball with and bounced relentlessly against the wall in your room until the neighbors complained; magic slates, jacks, and trucks of every description? Some of these toys are still around, thank goodness, though they take a back seat to Repugnus, the Transformer, and Scourge, and Cyclonus and Voltan; to Yomega—the yoyo with a brain (in my day it was the yo-yoer who was supposed to have the brain); to "Disect an Alien," which exhorts youngsters to "pull out the alien's organs, dripping in glowing blood—then try to put em back." Ugh! The more ghastly it seems, the better. Nevertheless, on a recent trip to a toy store I was relieved to see that Mr. Potato Head was still around although he had grown a little older and had produced a family of potato heads, and that Barbie was very much in evidence. To her credit Barbie had moved up in life and was now living in a posh town house and sporting a wardrobe that would make Elizabeth Taylor envious. Between you and me I think Barbie and Donald Trump have something going. How else could she afford all those clothes?

But enough of this. You want to know what's on the drawing board for the future, what wonderful toys we can look forward to that will keep our children from becoming bored? Here then a preview:

FOR THE BABY SET:

GUM CHUM—Gum Chum is a chewable, indestructible doll that baby can rend to his heart's delight without destroying either Gum Chum or himself. It also soothes Baby's gums with a harmless anesthetic while playing hit tunes from *Sesame Street*. Gum Chum tastes like Daddy's leg, Baby's favorite flavor, though it also comes in other gamey flavors like Mommy's leg, Grandma's hand, Puppy's dish, and shoe.

GIRLS' TOYS
DOLLS:

REAL BABY—The newest trend in dolls will be the marketing of real babies. They are expensive and take nine months to produce, but they are worth it. They wet their pants, the carpet, the bed, and everything else. They say, "Mama, Mama," until they drive you to distraction, but only after about eighteen months. You can comb their hair, wash them, feed them, and in every way treat them as real babies. Their only drawback is that they tend to grow so that when your daughter is in college, "Real Baby" will probably be in high school and starting litigation against you for child support. Maybe you can marry her off.

YUPPIE DOLLS—Ted, Marv, Gary, and Wayne. These yuppie dolls, each of whom is successful in a different field: Wall Street, real estate, insurance, or greenmail, all drive Mercedes cars and live in condos in fashionable neighborhoods. In the main they do better than you or anyone in your family. In fact they do so well that you would like your daughter to marry one of them. Unfortunately, they do not want to marry your daughter, since they've been sleeping with her for years and think she's a slut. Sorry about that. Maybe she could clean up her act.

DOLL'S DOLLS—One of the latest trends in dolls, is a whole array of dolls for your dolls. Thus it is high time you bought Barbie a doll of her own. Maybe you could buy her a Jennifer doll which is just like Barbie only much smaller (doll's doll size), and has a modern name befitting a doll of today. Other doll's dolls are Alexa, Alison, Lisa, Megan, and Kay Kay.

JEWELRY—Wide selection from Van Cleef & Arpels, Tiffany, Cartier, Bailey Banks & Biddle.

BOYS' TOYS:

SMELLBOTS—Smellbots are incredible robots that look like the fiercest of intergalactic warriors but smell like pizza, and Big Mac's, and Ring Dings, and you guessed it, they are entirely edible. Thus once your smellbot has destroyed its target enemy or whatever you program him to attack, you can eat him. Here comes one now, ummmm!

INVISIBLE—You just take the tablet with a glass of water, and . . .

Unbelievable, right? All the guys are doing it.

GRUNCHO, THE MAGNIFICENT—Metal eating monster from the planet Monoxidyl—loves nothing more than devouring swords, guns, knives or other primitive metal weapons used by superheroes from Earth. Gargantuan appetite for metal, virtually insatiable.

DECAP-A-FOE—A truly macho ninja warrior sword made of maidenhair damascus steel and sharpened with safety in mind so that it can only cut through bank vaults. Decap-a-Foe is designed for youngsters twelve to eighteen to hew down forests, slice onions, or decapitate any alien within ten light years of his room.

Warning: Not to be used in the presence of Gruncho, The Magnificent.

UNISEX TOYS:

TOTALMAN—Totalman is a complete wearable sensory eco-system, designed for adolescents who wish to tune out their parents and the rest of the world. It provides music, fragrances, and visual effects for the user. The youngster simply steps into the Totalman and zips it up from the inside. Within seconds, he or she is transported into a fabulous kaleidoscopic world of bright colors, animal rhythms, and exotic and intoxicating fragrances from which he never wants to leave. It is only at suppertime that a hard rap on the head from a sibling usually reminds him that it is time to climb out of Totalman for dinner.

29

DOES JOGGING CAUSE WARTS?

Just as evidence begins to accumulate that jogging and other aerobic regimens might, in fact, help us stave off heart disease, not to mention old age and flagging spirits, comes word that these same strenuous exercises may increase the risk of developing warts.

Does jogging cause warts, you know, the ugly kind that cover your face and body and make you look like a cauliflower? Some researchers think so.

According to Dr. Havelock Pelloponesian, Professor of Surface Blemishes at the University of Michigan:

"The more we research, the clearer it becomes that there is a direct connection between jogging and warts. I mean, have you ever seen the perspiration and gunk that adheres to the face of a serious jogger? Especially in the city. This stuff clogs up the pores and produces warts. There's no question about it. People who have jogged for years look like old logs with fungus growing all over them. I, personally, can't stand to look at them before dinner. They're disgusting. Yuck! Here comes one now, get me out of here."

Dr. Pelloponesian is not the only one to link jogging with warts. Joe "The Toad" feels his warts are directly attributable to jogging.

"See these warts, man? They came from jogging. You know what I mean? Like that's how I got them, man, from jogging."

"Sure, Joe, I understand, your warts came from jogging."

"That's right, man. I got these warts from jogging. Now everybody thinks I'm bad luck. Ya know what I mean, man?"

"Yeah, I know what you mean, Joe, jogging caused your warts. Shit, I just touched you. I'm gonna have bad luck now for years. Damn!"

"That's okay, man. I know the antidote. Just say after me . . . rain, rain, go away, come again another day. . . ."

"Isn't that for rain, Joe?"

"Yeah, yeah, you're right that's for rain. Sorry. You're gonna have bad luck for years now."

It is interesting to note that despite what Joe "The Toad" says, other joggers have described his style of running as hopping, not jogging. So the likelihood that his warts are unrelated to jogging exists.

"He may just be ugly," says one unbeliever, "but there's no question that he's bad luck. He touched a friend of mine once, and the guy's had nothing but trouble since. His wife left him. He lost all his money. His house caved in. And he's been given only a few months to live. But there's nothing really to worry about. Just don't get close enough where he can touch you, and you'll be okay."

What about the man on the street, does he think jogging causes warts?

"You bet it does. Every time you come down hard on the pavement another wart forms. If you run two or three miles a day, you can get several thousand warts in an afternoon."

"And you, sir?"

"Yeah, I agree. Jogging causes warts. I knew those runners were nuts. Now I know why. They get warts."

Like prickly heat, warts from jogging is spreading fast. Even though warts are believed to develop in and of themselves from jogging, they are also known to be communicable. As the joggers run along paths and tracks, bumping into each other, they spread the dread affliction. And hop-toads like Joe are the worst of all. Unfortunately it is difficult to tell from a distance if another runner has warts, or even if he is a toad. You have to get up real close, and usually by that time it's too late, he's bumped into you.

"Sorry, did I bump into you?"

"Yes, you did. Now what do I do?"

"I'd get to a doctor fast, if I were you."

Prevention may be the best way of countering the spread of warts, say the experts.

"I'd wear the thickest clothing I had, if I were running," says Dr. Miles Lylekin, of Johns Hopkins Running Disease Center. "Heavy flannels, and wools, even if it was the summer. Anything to protect against the warts." Most runners seem to be sticking to this advice. On any given day you can see them in the park, and along the byways, arrayed in the most outlandish running outfits, body stockings and even armor. The armor seems the most ridiculous of all, "clank, clank, screetch, clank." But no warts.

Meanwhile researchers are working feverishly to develop a vaccine that joggers can take to prevent warts. If they are successful, joggers will once again be able to breathe easy and go back to just being a nuisance.

÷
30
÷

I WONDER
WHAT EVER
HAPPENED TO?

Generally speaking here in New York, people divide into two classes: those who are curious about what has become of their friends and schoolmates from the past, and those who are not. I fall into the former category. As I approach the venerable age of fifty from its underside, I burn with nostalgic curiosity about my companions of yore. What do they look like? Who is successful, who is not? I want to know what ever happened to Big Earl from West 96th Street who could fell a grizzly bear with one blow from his mighty fist, and whether in "real life" he has turned into a professional football player, an insurance salesman, or a bouncer at the Hard Rock Café, or is he just spending his time punching out bears like the old days. And where is sultry, super sexy, Mary Jo McGilligan, the six-foot head cheerleader, who was a cross between Marilyn Monroe and L'il Abner's Daisy Mae, only bigger and better, and who reputedly entertained the entire football team behind the grandstand late one Saturday afternoon? I have been dutifully looking for her on movie screens and Broadway stages and on the TV for years now, waiting for her to surface, expecting that sooner or later she would be discovered and share her charms with the American public. Is it possible the CIA found her first and has been using her as a strategic weapon to extract secrets from the KGB? Or did she finally settle down after all was said and done with Mick "The Bone" DiCagliaro, her black-leather-jacketed boyfriend, and leader of "The Satans" from whom everyone tried to save her (he would amount to nothing, he had pimples, he killed people for fun) to no avail? I recently heard a rumor that Mick "The Bone" is now the CEO of a giant octopus conglomerate whose tentacles extend halfway around the globe. That he has fabulous homes in Paris, London, Palm Beach, as well as a triplex penthouse atop Trump Tower. Maybe Mary Jo made the right decision after all.

Still I can understand the reluctance of some people to actively seek out friends or classmates from the past. They wish to remember these individuals as they were, to etch them in their memories with their kinks and their idiosyncrasies, the way they looked, the way they acted, thirty or forty years ago, never to change. They have made new friends over the years and new lives—they do not wish to let the past intrude into the present. And with justification.

Not long ago I stopped with my wife to have lunch on

Madison Avenue. Three pleasant but matronly ladies sat down at the very next table and began to converse in conspiratorial tones, all the while casting glances in our direction. At first I thought perhaps something was amiss with our clothing or that I had dropped a fork on the floor when one of the ladies suddenly addressed me saying:

"Lewis? Lewis Frumkes?"

To which I replied, "Yes, I am Lewis Frumkes, do I know you?"

After a flurry of giggles, the lady answered, "Lewis, don't you recognize us, I'm Arlene, and that's Susan, and this is Linda."

"Omigod!" I exclaimed, "Of course I do. How are you? What have you been up to all these years?"

And indeed I was delighted and excited about this chance meeting if surprised by their appearance. While they were not unattractive ladies, they little resembled the girls I remembered. They were middle-aged women, heavier than when I knew them, with hair that was either gray or turning gray. Each had married a lawyer or doctor and had children now that were older than we were when we had last seen each other. After having introduced the girls to my wife, Arlene, Susan, Linda and I spent a few moments reminiscing about the fifties and finding out who of the gang any of us had run into recently or still kept in contact with. Then we said we'd be in touch and went back to our respective conversations knowing full well that it would not be, that our lives had sufficiently diverged for better or for worse, so that the past could never again be recaptured or conjured up as anything more than but a temporary illusion.

And then the following week I ran into Beverly on the street. Beverly, my confidant from thirty-five years ago with whom I had had marathon telephone conversations while my parents were out, for seven and eight hours at a time. Beverly who knew me better than any psychoanalyst ever could, to whom I had confessed my darkest and deepest secrets— that I really did love Jina M, even though she didn't know it—that I was furious with Billy B for daring to even look on her—that my I.Q. had been revealed to me in a dream, and it was 323. Beverly who understood me and made me laugh, and feel better, and with whom I had playfully even petted once or twice under the guise of good friendship and then gently slipped my hand under her skirt. This Beverly didn't even recognize me. And when I physically stopped her and expressed my joy at having bumped into her, she tried to rush past me, and told me she was late for a meeting with her spiritualist, and was running low on drugs, and was I into, like, coke? And the truth is she looked worse than she sounded, and she sounded awful, and I regretted our meeting, and cursed the fates, and resolved to let the past stay buried.

That was until I received a letter in the mail the other day about a forthcoming thirty-year high school reunion. And I found myself musing about Wicked Emily, and Walter, and Socky, and Eddie Brown and wondering what they were all doing, and whom they might have married, and what each of them probably looks like today. And soon I was sending back the reply card saying, "Yes, I'd be happy to attend," and recalling my blind crush on Merry what's-her-name who became Miss Rheingold, and my best friend writing in my yearbook, "In the golden chain of friendship, regard me as a link," and thinking lasciviously, what the devil ever happened to Mary Jo McGilligan?

$$\frac{\bullet}{31}$$

SOME SUGGESTIONS FOR THE "EDUCATION" PRESIDENT

It is not enough for George Bush just to declare that he is the "Education" President. As the new Chief of State he must actually get out there in the pedagogical fields with exciting programs to turn the country around. If he does not introduce imaginative legislation and viable solutions to campus problems, the U.S. will soon fall behind first the Japanese, then the Swedes, and the Soviets, and finally even the Balinese in terms of educating its citizenry. Dumb citizens do not accomplish anything; an educated citizenry is the key to a rich and productive future.

Here are some suggestions to help President Bush fulfill his campaign promises:

1. HANG DELINQUENT STUDENTS

Recent studies have shown that there is a growing crime problem in our schools. Students not only steal from one another they steal from faculty members and security guards as well. They also vandalize campus buildings every chance they get. Just why they do these things is anybody's guess, but some theorists believe it has to do with a deficiency of vitamin A. Whatever the reason, it is clear that we must hang these students. Headlines such as "HARVARD HANGS FIRST STUDENT" will serve as an effective deterrent to other students contemplating rowdy or disruptive behavior. If it does not, "HARVARD HANGS ALL OF ITS STUDENTS" is certain to work.

2. MASSAGE STUDENTS' HEADS

It is a well-known fact that massaging one's head not only brings it up to room temperature but raises the I.Q. as well. Therefore, the President should mandate a head massage program in all high schools at once. Licensed masseuses can easily be lured into education by offering them $600,000 a year, or half of what they are presently making.

With higher I.Q.s from massage, students should show immediate results, such as the increased ability to do crossword puzzles and repair their own CD players. This will ameliorate our much tarnished educational image worldwide.

3. STUDENTS SHOULD SLEEP WITH BOOKS UNDER THEIR PILLOWS

A simple procedure which will not use precious funds allocated for other programs is to have students sleep with their books under their pillows. Since time immemorial educators have been aware that students who sleep with books under their pillows learn more than other students. This is because the knowledge contained in the books seeps into their heads during the night while they are sleeping. Legion are the cases of empty-headed students who wake up the next morning biology geniuses. The larger the books, the more that is absorbed. President Bush should insist that students sleep with their books under their pillows immediately.

4. COURSE MATERIALS SHOULD BE RELEVANT

The surgeon walks into the OR to prepare for open heart surgery. Does he think, "Now let's see, what would Jane Eyre have done? Would she have anesthetized the patient first?" No, *Jane Eyre* is a novel, a made up piece of fiction by Charlotte Brontë. It has nothing to do with open heart surgery and is, therefore, useless to the surgeon. Nor did General George Patton find much use for *Jane Eyre* when he was facing Rommel's tanks in North Africa. In fact chances are *Jane Eyre* won't help you much either when you get in the ring against Mike Tyson, unless you are also carrying a 60 millimeter Howitzer with elephant bullets. President Bush must eliminate *Jane Eyre* from our educational system now, before she totally wrecks it.

5. AUCTION OFF GRADES

One of the major problems facing the Bush administration is how to raise monies to finance the educational programs. I believe the president should auction off grades. There are many wealthy parents who are desperate to get their kids into good schools. No harm done if Bancroft Harding III purchases a few A's for Banky IV at $100,000 each. These are extra A's manufactured exclusively for fund-raising purposes, not taken away from someone else. Banky IV is going to own The Cliff & Murchison Bank when he gets out of college; he needs some help. With the auction option nobody gets hurt and lots of money pours in. I figure $10,000,000,000 can be raised at auction and funneled into education.

6. REDUCE THE NUMBER OF STUDENTS GOING TO SCHOOL

Clearly there are too many students going to school. The system is overloaded. Classrooms are stuffed and crowded. There is not enough food to go around in lunchrooms. If some of the students aren't pruned out of the system at once, it will choke. But how? Bold policies are called for and hard decisions must be made, that's how. No more kids with blue eyes, for example, is a good way to begin. No more kids who pick their noses. No more kids who smell like peanut butter. All kids whose first names begin with "S," out. Kids with blond hair, also out. Anyone who has slept with Emily, out. These rules may seem arbitrary and unfair, but they will work. It takes a president with courage to institute these rules. I believe George Bush has that courage.

7. A NEW MOTTO

President Bush must show leadership by creating a new motto for education, one that can be sung out loud, worn on T-shirts, sky-written across the heavens. Come to think of it, he already has. He has created a motto that teachers can use to advantage with their students in almost any situation. READ MY LIPS! You've got to love a president who can come up with a motto like that.

The educational system in the U.S. can be révivified. George Bush can do it. Take my suggestions, George. READ MY LIPS!

32

SOME
OF MY
PSEUDONYMS

Just as Doris Lessing has attempted to dramatize the difficulties faced by unknown writers by submitting two novels herself under the pseudonym of Jane Somers, so I have tried to show how easy it is for well-known writers to get published and sold by turning out dozens of works under famous names. For example, one of my novels, *Tough Guys Don't Dance*, published under one of my pseudonyms, Norman Mailer, made several best-seller lists and reaped a fortune.

When I submitted it five years ago under its original title, *Rocky, the Wallflower,* Random House rejected it posthaste.

Another of my books, *Poland,* written under the nom de plume James Michener, has also done extremely well, while *Bulgaria,* submitted under my real name, has yet to be sold.

And how about my book *Mistral's Daughter,* which I published under Judith Krantz and which was made into a TV special? Do you really suppose it would have had a chance as *That Painter's Girl* under my name? No way! Nor, for that matter would *Pet Sematary* have done so well had I tried to market it under *When Bad Things Happen to Good Dogs* and used my own name instead of Stephen King.

For the record, at last count I have also written books as Bernard Malamud, John Updike, Alice Adams, Saul Bellow, Harold Robbins, William Styron, Russell Baker (yes, I write humor too) and dozens of others, including all the works by Lessing not written by Lessing herself as Jane Somers. By splitting the royalties and letting the writers in on my experiment, I have kept them from exposing me and have made them and myself millions in the process.

33

SCONCE CONTROL AND THE TOASTER HARVEST

Most people have no idea where anything comes from and just assume that everything is manufactured by hot companies in southern California. In fact nothing could be farther from the truth.

There are many sources other than hot companies in southern California where things come from and I am constantly staggered by the amount of misinformation about origins. Thus it seems imperative to set the record straight. Take these common household objects for example:

TOASTERS

Toasters grow on vines in the Deep South: Alabama, Louisiana, and Mississippi. When they are ripe the farmers pluck them off the vines and ship them to hardware and appliance stores up North where they are sold as shower gifts for prospective brides. The best toasters, which weren't around when I was a kid, are the hybrid toaster-ovens the result of crossing conventional vine-grown toasters with small kitchen ovens.

END TABLES

For years when coffee tables and drop-leafs would spawn, their offspring, the so-called end tables, would be discarded or used for chopping blocks out in the garden. Today, end tables are considered perfectly acceptable for finishing off corners of living and bed rooms, or bracketing sofas. So ubiquitous have they become, in fact, that interior designers and room planners are giving serious thought to having all new coffee tables altered.

ASHTRAYS

Like meteorites, ashtrays come from outer space. They originate in space as small spherical objects and travel through the galaxies at incredible speeds. While no one knows for sure just how they are formed, we do know that once they enter the earth's atmosphere they split in half and polish themselves on the way down, eventually to be gathered up by prospectors and sold to gift and department stores. The best ashtrays have stardust imbedded in their surfaces.

SCONCES

Sconces grow on walls like toadstools and must either be cut away where they are not wanted, or treated with chemicals. "Sconce-Away" is perhaps the most widely used of the fungicides and least toxic to other wall hangings. The curious thing about sconces is that unlike ceiling fixtures, they seem always to grow in pairs.

MOTHBALLS

Mothballs are laid by giant camphor moths that lay as many as two or three hundred balls at a time. Rarely found in the West, mothballs must be imported from Japan and Taiwan, where the camphor moths prefer to nest. Recently, the Japanese Government, in recognition of more than 3,000 years with no holes in their sweaters, declared the camphor moth the national insect of Japan.

MIRRORS

Mirrors are mined in quarries like mica-schist. They are sedimentary and composed of thousands of layers that must be separated by expensive precision machinery and polished before being looked into. Recently one careless individual looked into an unseparated mirror and was crushed to death by his own reflection before being turned to stone. Mirrors, while hypnotic, are hardly play toys.

TELEPHONES

Telephones are small electronic animals that were first used by Greek generals during the Trojan War to carry messages back to their girlfriends in Athens. "Hi Honey, you won't believe this giant wooden horse we're building to smuggle soldiers into Troy. Really awesome. Miss you baby, kiss kiss." Named after "Phonathon," the Greek god of fund raising, telephones can be found today in virtually every multimouth household, from New York to San Francisco. And while they are relatively care free, a little pat on the receiver now and then can go a long way.

LIGHT BULBS

Light bulbs grow on electric trees in the marshes and bayous of the Gulf Coast states and are shipped to other regions in corrugated cardboard containers. Of course I am talking about 15-, 25- and 30-watt bulbs, which are the only bulbs grown domestically. For big 200-watters and spots, the United States as well as the rest of the world must import their bulbs from Brazil where the largest electric trees grow. To knowledgeable bulb fanciers everywhere Brazilian bulbs are like Belgian chocolates: they represent the best that money can buy.

CLUB CHAIRS

Club chairs, as you may have imagined, are hand-fashioned from clubs, the same kind that your great-great-grandmother used to use to klop your great-great-grandfather over the head when he got out of line. The reason the chairs are so costly is that very few clubs of the sort your great-great-grandmother used exist anymore now that people have learned to communicate with one another through lawyers.

It should now be clear that the objects in our homes have far more interesting and exotic origins than most of us had hitherto suspected, and as a consequence, we should treat them with more care. After all, when an ashtray has traveled over a billion light years from the Crab nebula just to sit on an end table, it really deserves our respect.

÷ 34 ÷

HOW
WILL
YOU
DIE?

You will most likely die from heart disease, cancer, or stroke, at the moment our leading causes of death. It was not always so. Years ago you were more likely to be struck down by bubonic plague, tuberculosis, or a club, depending on when and where you lived. Come to think of it a club may still get you in certain neighborhoods, but that's another story. However, dying from nuclear fallout in eighteenth century

France was virtually out of the question and people felt reassured knowing that.

Since you already know how you will probably die, perhaps you will feel reassured learning some of the ways you will probably not die. According to thanatologists, the chances of dying in the following ways are remote. (Though you never know, you could get lucky!)

242—You will win the lottery for $8,000,000 and drop dead.

320—Your memory will go, and you will forget that you are alive.

346—You will be swallowed by a giant hummingbird. (see #1,046)

1,046—You will be swallowed by a prune pit.

413—You will die from sexual exhaustion, the result of prolonged contact with the Dallas Cowboy Cheerleaders or the Dallas Cowboys, depending upon your preference.

428—While traveling to Palm Beach on vacation, you will be sucked out of the plane and into a black hole.

530—You choke on a Boeing 747.

553—You pull a hangnail and proceed to unravel.

574—You attempt to make Ripley's, *Believe It or Not*

by diving off the World Trade Tower into a marshmallow.

610—While visiting a sick aunt in the hospital, you are pulled into the catheter by an undertow and drown.

622—While reading a new novel, the type suddenly jumps off the page and eats you.

673—You are crushed under your own foot.

727—You contract converse disease and turn inside out.

792—After an attack of masochism, you volunteer to be a tackling dummy for the Washington Redskins. Even the team of micro surgeons from Baylor University Hospital cannot put you back together again.

802—At a press conference you kick Mike Tyson in the teeth.

814—During your metallic phase, you inadvertantly get wet and rust to death.

860—You plug your nose into the wrong electrical socket and are electrocuted.

$$\frac{\bullet}{35}$$

IN SEARCH
OF THE BEST
OVERLOOKED
PRIVATE
SCHOOLS

Every year, thousands of new sets of parents are confronted with the problem of both choosing and being chosen by one of the select group of private secondary schools. They want the best possible education for their children, no matter the cost.

This year, being no different from any other, they will descend, like lemmings, on the schools, to compete for the limited number of spaces available.

Having rejected public schools as a viable alternative, these parents will do exhaustive studies of the comparative merits of the private schools in their area. They will arm themselves with formidable and socially impeccable names to drop. They will rehearse little Saffron and Apollo for their interview till the kids wet their pants with anxiety. Sorry are the parents who fail in the quest for the holy grail of acceptance at the private school of their choice. They will hang their heads in shame, become social pariahs, perhaps attempt suicide.

To help the harried parents in their time of travail, I have briefly sketched some of the more outstanding and overlooked secondary institutions of learning, so that they may better make the match between school and child. God help them.

MISS FINSTER'S SCHOOL

An all-girls' school, Miss Finster's is both traditional and reactionary in its approach to education. Miss Finster, who founded the school in 1857, and who continues to serve as its headmistress despite outside pressures, believes that a proper student should come from a proper background. In consonance with this educational belief, neither E.R.B. nor other diagnostic evaluation tests are required for admission. While Miss Finster's is nondemoninational, documentation must be provided showing that a child's ancestors came to this country on either the *Mayflower* or the *Welcome*.

At Miss Finster's, special attention is given to teaching the girls voice modulation and mastery of understatement in all things.

THE COUNTRY ANIMAL SCHOOL

This all-boys school located on four hundred sprawling acres in the Ozarks, is dedicated to the proposition that an animal is man's best friend and vice versa.

The Country Animal School provides the boys with their first meaningful contact with farm animals. The boys feed, bathe, and sleep with the animals. While emotional bonds do inevitably form between the boys and the animals, the school does not actively encourage these relationships.

Many of the students go on to become zoologists, veterinarians, and singing cowboys. Hitherto, the school has featured a course in animal husbandry.

Each of the two hundred or so students enrolled in the school is charged with cherishing his animal, in sickness and in health, until the semester ends, when they do part.

Tuition of $3,000 includes room, board, and feed.

LIB

Lib is a coed school of ethnic, sexual, and preferential diversity. It attracts activist students from every walk of life, and trains them not only to speak out, but to strike out.

The curriculum offers courses in counter-establishment revolution, protest tactics, and sloganeering.

Unfortunately, there will be no classes this semester, as the school burned down.

MARTINET

Martinet is a very selective and old-fashioned school with emphasis on discipline. According to headmistress Monique

Von Cleef, the girls are expected to wear the traditional all leather school uniform, as well as seven (count them, one, two, three, four, five, six, **seven**) inch high-heeled boots. The curriculum closely follows the heuristic principles of Kraft-Ebing as laid down in *Psychopathia Sexualis*.

Admission to Martinet is strict, as is everything else about this program. An E.R.B. stress test for tissue tolerance is required, and easy bleeders are discouraged from applying. Martinet has two hundred highly motivated students.

THE GALTON SCHOOL

The Galton School is the most highly selective school in the country. An I.Q. in excess of 180 is mandatory for admission as well as 800 SAT scores and concrete evidence of gifted-ness, such as a Nobel or Pulitzer prize. Galton offers courses in modern algebra and topology, and seminars in relativity theory and quantum mechanics. Students may choose from sixty foreign languages, including seven dialects of Sanskrit. In the past, students have often created their own languages, making use of mathematical logics and algorithms.

At present, the student body consists of one pupil, hence, there is an excellent student-teacher ratio.

BABBITT

Babbitt is a traditional school with a middle-of-the-road phi-losophy and curriculum. While Babbitt accepts intelligent and minority students, it prefers Norman Rockwell kids of average ability who aspire to middle management positions and gray flannel suits. Students are expected to conform to the expectations and values of the school both in and out of class. Uniforms are *de rigueur*.

As one might expect, tuition at Babbitt is average.

THE FAR-OUT RAMAYANA EDUCATION AND KINKY YESHIVA

The Far-Out Ramayana Education and Kinky Yeshiva or FREAKY, as it is acronymically known, is a progressive school. It offers courses in obscurantist philosophy and the cults of the "now" generation.

Emphasis is placed on spiritual development through experimental use of Hylozoism, Voodoo, and other arcane psychic disciplines.

The admission policy at Freaky is sometimes selective, sometimes not, depending on swings in mood.

Tuition is subordinated to oneness.

LOFTY

Located in a townhouse with walnut-paneled elevators and Sherle Wagner bathrooms, Lofty offers a cushy education for a somewhat plutocratic student body. The curriculum features classes in "voluptuary hedonism," "eudemonics," and "managing one's own trust." Extracurricular activities include Yachting, Petropolis, and Polo. The school has a crack Petropolis team.

Admission to Lofty is determined only by one's ability to pay the tuition, which is fifty thousand dollars per semester. Transportation to and from the school by chauffeured Rolls is provided for at an additional cost of five thousand dollars. Lofty is coed.

36

FATHER'S
TURN

My son Tim is just like any other healthy seven-year-old boy: faster than a speeding bullet, able to leap tall buildings in a single bound, more powerful than a locomotive, and easily twice as noisy. He also goes to school on those mornings when I am feeling up to it.

The reason I say when I am feeling up to it is because getting him off to school is not unlike preparing an Apollo rocket for moon launch—only slightly more difficult. Let's examine one of those mornings and perhaps we will discover where I am going wrong.

7 A.M.: The alarm goes off just two hours after I successfully convince Tim that the eerie glow filtering into his room at 5 A.M. is the sun and not a death ray from some alien space ship balancing on his window sill. However, I am now convinced that the blinding light threatening to separate my eyelids is, in fact, the death ray from some alien space ship. I close my eyes for exactly one minute's sleep.

7:30 A.M.: The extra minute is up and I bolt out of bed with full knowledge that I have overslept. Quickly I wash my face and brush my teeth, put on a robe, and make for Tim's room.

7:31 A.M.: I enter Tim's room and find that he is still sleeping peacefully, a ray gun in one hand and a football helmet enclosing his head. I knock on the helmet gently but no one is home. I knock again. Faint stirrings. "Time to get up," I say. A voice from within the helmet says "Zzzzzzzzzzzzzz." I pull the shades and the room comes alive with light and noises from the street. From behind me a wee voice says, "C'mon Dad, pull down the shade, you're hurting my eyes." (Notice I am hurting his eyes.) "Time to get up," I repeat, "school." "Oh, no" comes the enthusiastic reply.

7:35 A.M.: I retreat to the kitchen to fix breakfast and promptly drop an egg on my foot.

7:36 A.M.: I return to Tim's room where he has managed to sit up. I lay out his clothes and urge him to hurry and dress. I might just as well ask the chair to hurry and dress.

7:37 A.M.: I rush back to the kitchen and prepare Tim's favorite breakfast, sugar laced with cold cereal and milk. I fill a glass with orange juice and place it on the breakfast table. I also include a vitamin pill in case his bowl of sugar is lacking any essential nutrients.

7:45 A.M.: I peer into Tim's room and discover to my amazement that he already has one sock in his hand. At this rate he will be dressed in time for dinner. I elect to help him. Carefully I follow him around the room getting a piece of clothing on each time he breaks stride.

7:55 A.M.: Tim and the table divide his breakfast. The table gets the larger share. The floor gets a little too.

7:57 A.M.: Tim retrieves his homework from under his bed and neatly squashes it into his pocket. He fills his knapsack with assorted school implements: a water pistol, three rubber bands, two metal screws, and a Captain something or other comic book, then heads for the door.

I say "Have a good day."

He says, "   ."

Fortunately, I already know that I exist so I don't feel quite as bad.

8: A.M.: The bus arrives and Tim chooses a good seat near the exhaust pipe. As the bus begins to pull away I see another kid hit him over the head with a baseball bat and I know that he has made a friend. I trudge back to the bedroom and get under the covers with my wife.

Too late I feel something warm and soft lying under me. Oh yes, Tim has a little sister, Amber, who also goes to school—now it is her turn.

"Daddy, you're sitting on me," she whines disconsolately.

"So I am," I answer.

"Get off, Daddy."

"Okay, okay," I say, removing myself from the bed.

"Daddy, I want breakfast."

"Come with me, Honey, we'll go into the kitchen."

"No, Daddy, bring it to me in bed."

"In bed?" I shriek, mildly surprised by this royal request.

"Mommy always brings me breakfast in bed," argues my daughter.

"She does?" I ask incredulously.

"Yes, Daddy, and I want *those* eggs."

"Which eggs?" I inquire.

"The ones Mommy makes."

"Scrambled eggs?"

"No."

"Fried eggs?"

"No."

"Soft-boiled eggs?"

"No."

"Well, what kind then," I ask, raising my voice ever so slightly.

"You know, Daddy, the kind Mommy makes."

Suddenly, I am back where I started and beginning to feel ill. I walk slowly over to where my wife is sleeping and gaze down at her lovely, untroubled face. She had been up half the night making a chicken costume for Amber's school play and is now slumbering peacefully. I kiss her on the forehead, and then like a devil I wake her up.

ABOUT THE AUTHOR

Lewis Burke Frumkes writes and edits the Final Straw column for *Penthouse* magazine, hosts The Lewis Burke Frumkes radio show on WNWK in New York, and teaches at Marymount Manhattan College and Harvard University. In the seventh grade, at Albert Leonard Junior High School in New Rochelle, he was voted "Most Cheerful."